Sharing the Same Heart

Sharing the Same Heart:
Parents, Children, and Our Inherent Essence

Dharma Talks by Seon Master Daehaeng
English translation and editing by
Hanmaum International Culture Institute
Cover Design by Su Yeon Park
Published by Hanmaum Publications

First Edition: August, 2017

within Korea
tel: (031)470-3175 / fax: (031)470-3209
outside Korea
tel: (82-31)470-3175 / fax: (82-31)470-3209
E-mail: onemind@hanmaum.org

ISBN 978-89-91857-48-3 (03220)

국립중앙도서관 출판예정도서목록(CIP)

Sharing the same heart : parents, children, and our inherent
essence / Dharma talks by Seon Master Daehaeng ;
English translation and editing by Hanmaum International
Culture Institute. -- [Anyang] : Hanmaum publications,
2017
　　p. ;　cm

Translated from Korean
ISBN 978-89-91857-48-3 03220 : US$15.00

225.2-KDC6
294.34-DDC23　　　　　　　　　CIP2017017377

A CIP catalogue record of the National Library of Korea
for this book is available at the homepage of CIP (http://
seoji.nl.go.kr) and Korean Library Information System
Network(http://www.nl.go.kr/kolisnet). (CIP2017017377)

Sharing the Same Heart

Parents, Children, and Our Inherent Essence

Seon Master Daehaeng

hanmaum

Contents

Ceaselessly Flowing

Flowing and flowing,
endless eons of flowing,
parents becoming children,
children becoming parents,
changing their shapes over and over,
how can words describe all of this?

Gathering together
according to how we've lived in the past,
according to the karmic affinity we've created,
and being born into this world,
with so many hardships in just a single season.
Every being is my parent,
everyone is my child.
Oh, this endless flowing,
connected altogether and ceaselessly changing.

Flowing and flowing,

endless eons of flowing,

changing our shapes over and over,

each time according to our last life.

How we lived becomes our karma,

the process of cause and effect forms our genes.

This body is like a house,

with so many beings living here altogether.

Take all those lives that are bothering you,

whether they come from the inside or outside,

accept them non-dually,

make them one,

and watch them surrender.

Discover what it means to be truly free,

with the power that comes from being

connected altogether and ceaselessly changing.

— Daehaeng Kun Sunim

One day I happened to meet Daehaeng Kun Sunim as she walked out into the main courtyard of the Seon Center. There were two or three young children playing there, chasing each other and yelling with abandon. They probably lived in the neighborhood, and had found a wide-open space for their games. But they were being kind of noisy in the heart of the temple, and one of the sunims with us grumbled about it.

But Kun Sunim spoke up, saying, "I think it's beautiful."

Even now, twenty years later, I still remember this.

It showed me an aspect beyond the surface, the noisy kids, beyond the temporary disruption, and nudged me towards a more complete picture. For play is a sign of healthy kids. It's good for them, and it's a pretty good world where kids have the time and energy, and safety, to run and shout.

There's an expression in Korean, that when the headwaters of a stream are clean, the water downstream will be as well. It flows from the top.

If the parents are working diligently at entrusting everything to the fundamental, awakened true nature within us, which is also the connection we all share, then as they get a sense of this, their connection with their children opens up and becomes more vibrant. The children in turn respond to this, and as this energy flows back and forth, parents have a better sense of what they need to be doing.

Thus, while Daehaeng Kun Sunim often encourages parents to teach their children about this practice of relying upon our foundation, she spends most of her time talking with the parents, encouraging them to work on their half of things.

To be honest, there's only so much parents can do. Children come into this world with their own personality, history, and karma. As any parent can testify, beyond a certain point, you can't really make children do much. Yelling and threatening are always temptations, but even when they yield results, everyone involved is often left feeling a little terrible.

Instead, as we begin to discover the light within us, our own inherent teacher, then we begin to get a better sense of the situation, and how to respond effectively. We begin to see what we can do to help bring forth this light in others. And as our own light begins to shine forth, children too begin to sense this. They learn from how we respond to them, but they also learn from how we treat others and how we respond to the things that come up in our life.

In addition to the need for parents to work on their own spiritual practice, Daehaeng Kun Sunim also answers questions in these Dharma talks about prenatal care and education, and specific issues between parents and children. Because fetuses and young children are changing so rapidly, the positive influences they receive at this time are magnified throughout their life, so to her, this was an excellent opportunity to help deepen a child's potential for spiritual growth.

When the energy of our own fundamental Buddha nature shines bright, then it can automatically connect with and support the people in our lives. And as children experience the taste of this energy, that becomes a standard, an idea of what's possible, and so they don't easily fall into dark paths. And while the topic of this book is children and parents, this is also true for the people around us.

When our hearts and spirits are bright, that light shines on everyone we encounter. And while we'll likely never know the effects of this, just by being in the world, we can be a source of hope and compassion for others, whether they be our children, parents, or just passing by on the sidewalk.

May all beings realize this light for themselves, and awaken to its power, joy, and compassion.

with palms together,
The Hanmaum International Culture Institute
Buddha's Birthday, 2561 (2017 C.E.)

About Daehaeng Kun Sunim

Daehaeng *Kun Sunim*[1](1927-2012) was a rare teacher in Korea: a female *Seon(Zen)*[2] master, a nun whose students also included monks, and a teacher who helped revitalize Korean Buddhism by dramatically increasing the participation of young people and men.

She broke out of traditional models of spiritual practice to teach in such a way that allowed anyone to practice and awaken, making laypeople a particular focus of her efforts. At the same time, she was a major force for the advancement of *Bhikkunis*,[3] heavily supporting traditional nuns' colleges as well as the modern Bhikkuni Council of Korea.

---

1. Sunim / Kun Sunim: Sunim is the respectful title of address for a Buddhist monk or nun in Korea, and Kun Sunim is the title given to outstanding nuns or monks.

2. Seon(禪)(Chan, Zen)**:** Seon describes the unshakeable state where one has firm faith in their inherent foundation, their Buddha-nature, and so returns everything they encounter back to this fundamental mind. It also means letting go of "I," "me," and "mine" throughout one's daily life.

3. Bhikkunis: Female sunims who are fully ordained are called Bhikkuni(比丘尼) sunims, while male sunims who are fully ordained are called Bhikku(比丘) sunims. This can also be a polite way of indicating male or female sunims.

Born in Seoul, Korea, she awakened when she was around eight years old and spent the years that followed learning to put her understanding into practice. For years, she wandered the mountains of Korea, wearing ragged clothes and eating only what was at hand. Later, she explained that she hadn't been pursuing some type of asceticism; rather, she was just completely absorbed in entrusting everything to her fundamental *Buddha*[4] essence and observing how that affected her life.

Those years profoundly shaped Kun Sunim's later teaching style; she intimately knew the great potential, energy, and wisdom inherent within each of us, and recognized that most of the people she encountered suffered because they didn't realize this about themselves. Seeing clearly the great light in every individual, she taught people to rely upon this inherent foundation, and refused to teach anything that distracted from this most important truth.

---

4. Buddha: In this text, "Buddha" and "Bodhisattva" are capitalized out of respect, because these represent the essence and function of the enlightened mind. "The Buddha" always refers to Sakyamuni Buddha.

Without any particular intention to do so, Daehaeng Kun Sunim demonstrated on a daily basis the freedom and ability that arises when we truly connect with this fundamental essence inherent within us. The sense of acceptance and connection people felt from being around her, as well as the abilities she manifested, weren't things she was trying to show off. In fact, she usually tried to hide them because people would tend to cling to these, without realizing that chasing after them cannot lead to either freedom or awakening.

Nonetheless, in her very life, in everything she did, she demonstrated the freedom and ability that arises when we truly connect with this very basic, fundamental essence that we all have – that we are. She showed that because we are all interconnected, we can deeply understand what's going on with others, and that the intentions we give rise to can manifest and function in the world.

All of these are in a sense side effects, things that arise naturally when we are truly one with everyone and everything around us. They happen because we are able to flow in harmony with our world, with no dualistic views or attachments to get in the way. At this point, other beings are not cut off from us; they are another shape of ourselves. Who, feeling this to their very bones, could turn their back on others?

It was this deep compassion that made her a legend in Korea long before she formally started teaching. She was known for having the spiritual power to help people in all circumstances and with every kind of problem. She compared compassion to freeing a fish from a drying puddle, putting a homeless family into a home, or providing the school fees that would allow a student to finish high school. And when she did things like this, and more, few knew that she was behind it.

Her compassion was also unconditional. She would offer what help she could to individuals and organizations, whether they be Christian or Buddhist, a private organization or governmental. She would help nun's temples that had no relationship with her temple, Christian organizations that helped look after children living on their own, city-run projects to help care for the elderly, and much, much more. Yet, even when she provided material support, always there was the deep, unseen aid she offered through this connection we all share.

However, she saw that ultimately, for people to live freely and go forward in the world as a blessing to all around them, they needed to know about this bright essence that is within each of us. To help people discover this for themselves, she founded the first

Hanmaum[5] Seon Center in 1972. For the next forty years she gave wisdom to those who needed wisdom, food and money to those who were poor and hungry, and compassion to those who were hurting.

---

5. **Hanmaum**[han-ma-um]: "Han" means one, great, and combined, while "maum" means mind, as well as heart, and together they mean everything combined and connected as one. What is called "Hanmaum" is intangible, unseen, and transcends time and space. It has no beginning or end, and is sometimes called our fundamental mind. It also means the mind of all beings and everything in the universe connected and working together as one. In English, we usually translate this as "one mind."

Daehaeng Kun Sunim founded ten overseas branches of Hanmaum Seon Center, and her teachings have been translated into thirteen different languages to date: English, German, Russian, Chinese, French, Spanish, Indonesian, Italian, Japanese, Vietnamese, Estonian, and Czech, in addition to the original Korean. For more information about these or the overseas centers, please see the back of this book.

Dharma Talk 1

Faith in Action:
Learning to Rely upon Our Root

July 16, 1995

This talk was first published in English
as Volume 13 in the ongoing series,
Practice in Daily Life.

When I woke up this morning and heard the rain pouring down, I was worried about the people who would be sitting outside listening to the Dharma talk.[6] However, the rain has since stopped and I think it's because so many of you raised a sincere intention that it should.

Someone asked me, "Why are you only teaching people about using spiritual practice to solve problems in their daily life?"[7] Right? You've probably all heard something like this. However, the act of seeing something, hearing something, moving your body – all of this is the functioning of your foundation, your Buddha-nature. All of the interactions, all of the movement of everything in this world, including the universe itself, is the functioning of our foundation. There's no place this isn't true, and there's no time this hasn't been true.

So, when we try to shape and moderate our ordinary activities by relying upon our foundation, this itself is spiritual practice. When you respond to what you're seeing and hearing by giving rise to a

----

6. When Daehaeng Kun Sunim gave Dharma talks, it wasn't unusual for 5,000 or more people to attend. Because there weren't enough seats inside, many had to sit outside, listening to the talk through speakers.

7. There is a nuance of criticism for not focusing on "lofty" topics such as the sutras or "enlightenment."

wise thought and entrusting it to your foundation, this too is spiritual development. If we were to ignore the functioning of our fundamental *mind* [8] as it fills the world around us, how could any growth be possible?

The *Heart Sutra* says, "Form is emptiness, emptiness is form," doesn't it? This is what we've just been talking about: that everything is an interconnected whole, constantly flowing, where nothing remains fixed or unchanging. We are here today to learn this, and how we can apply this truth to our lives.

Right now, everything in your bodies is ceaselessly moving, and there's not a single part of this that isn't the functioning of your inherent nature. Even the blink of your eye is the functioning of your inherent nature. Living and breathing itself are the functioning of this nature. Because the Korean word for "functioning" also sounds like the word for "Dragon," people used the idea of "The Dragon Spirit" to represent the great power

---

8. Mind(心)(Kor. –maum)**:** In Mahayana Buddhism, "mind" refers to this fundamental mind, and almost never means the brain or intellect. It is intangible, beyond space and time, and has no beginning or end. It is the source of everything, and everyone is endowed with it.

that comes from this ceaseless manifesting. Yet if you take this flowing and moving whole, and try to understand it through your own fixed ideas and opinions, how could you make the least bit of progress in your practice?

We are able to live together as one with the universe because the foundation of our life is connected to the foundation of the universe. This is the source of life that exists within each of us. We can call this our essence, or our foundation, or our Buddha-nature, whatever you like. It isn't something that belongs to only a particular individual; rather, it flows through everything in the universe, and through it, all things and lives are connected. There's nothing that isn't part of this.

It's like how electric current can be split apart and transformed, and used in a thousand different ways to make our world a better place. Even in the air, even in the sky, things are changing and transforming through the energy of this Buddha-nature. Rain, snow, and wind all arise through this process.

We've gathered here today, as Dharma brothers and sisters, to learn how to make use of this fundamental energy and free ourselves. This is what the Buddha taught. But he also cautioned that if you get lost in analyzing things that inherently can't be split apart, you won't attain anything, nor will you be able to grow and develop.

There are a lot of sutras, aren't there? Such as the *Flower Ornament Sutra*, the *Lotus Sutra*, the *Thousand Hands Sutra*, and the *Heart Sutra*, which itself includes the deep meaning of all the other sutras. But the many things these sutras teach all arise from the same fundamental truth. It's all descriptions of the same thing. So, if we try to label or define everything in our daily life, as if they were separate things, how could we ever learn about this always-flowing foundation?

If you have a family, then you find yourself naturally switching between the role of a father, to a husband, to a brother, don't you? This is the way our fundamental *one mind*[9] functions – ceaselessly manifesting and changing according to needs and circumstances.

---

9. One mind: (Hanmaum [han-ma-um]) From the Korean, where "one" has a nuance of great and combined, while "mind" is more than intellect and includes "heart" as well. Together, they mean everything combined and connected as one. What is called "one mind" is intangible, unseen, and transcends time and space. It has no beginning or end, and is sometimes called our fundamental mind. It also means the mind of all beings and everything in the universe connected and working together as one.

This one mind, which can also be called Buddha, is within us, and is what enables everything to function together. Because this mind within us can give rise to intentions that are subtle and profound beyond imagining, it can be called Buddha. Because this mind can give rise to intentions beyond number, it is Buddha. Because this mind can see and hear anything, it is Buddha. Because of this mind, we are able to respond and manifest in any form needed, and so we are Buddha.

This ability to manifest and help beings evolve is so wondrous! Those who haven't experienced the amazing and beautiful ability of mind, those who haven't applied this ability and experienced its results, can't yet truly understand what's represented by ideas such as *"interdependent arising."* [10]

Nevertheless, because we are inherently endowed with these abilities, it's actually not that hard to make use of them. The reason people can't freely use them is because they're ignoring their true self. They don't have faith in it.

---

10. Interdependent arising, also known as **dependent arising:** The idea that all things arise according to, or are dependent upon, other things.

It's like a bean sprout ignoring the seed it's growing out of. Does it make sense for the transient sprout to ignore its source? That seed is eternal. I'm not talking about just bean seeds; this is true of the fundamental essence of all life, which is inherent within each of us. Yet, it's also true that the two have something in common. With just one bean seed, you can feed countless people, and still have seeds left over to feed people going forward, forever.

Similarly, this energy within us, this Buddha-nature, is eternal – it doesn't increase or decrease. Even if the entire human race died off, this energy wouldn't disappear. Although we die and that energy scatters, it isn't destroyed; it just scatters and then gathers together again, giving rise to other life. It gives rise to beings with bodies, and it gives rise to the wind, for that, too, is alive. Rain is alive, snow is alive, and flowing water, too, is a form of life.

All things are alive with this energy, and through it all the different manifestations that fill this world are connected and function together as a whole. This energy, this power, bursts forth with such infinite and incredible ability, and enables all life to grow and develop in so many different ways. It's this power that enables us to reach our ultimate goal.

Although everyone has this great energy and ability, many of you tend to think of yourselves as powerless, or that you can't do things well, or that you deserve to suffer because of the things you've done. So instead of using this infinite ability within you, you think you have to go off and bow or chant in proportion to your misdeeds.

However, these kinds of thoughts are actually blocking you. They prevent you from using your own inherent ability. If you're using your own mind to block your ability, do you think you'll be able to grow and evolve? No!

Above all else, you have to know your fundamental mind, and how to make use of it! You've made it to the level of a human being, so don't dare finish this life without knowing this. Then you can keep evolving. If people ignore their fundamental mind and just try to live without awakening to it, how are they different from animals?

Secondly, once you know about your fundamental mind, you need to have faith in its ability and try to apply that to your daily life. You need to know about this, because it's the only way to maintain the health of your body and your mind, and it's also the only way to take a large step forward in your evolution. This is also how everything you do can become a light for others.

This fundamental mind of yours is Buddha, so looking for Buddha outside yourself is exactly the same as leaving your house empty. Imagine if you've gone out somewhere and left your house unlocked, with the doors wide open. Anybody who wanders by can just go in and help themselves to whatever they want, can't they? They can break things, leave a mess, and basically destroy the place. And with no one there, the house begins to fill with bugs and spider webs, and slowly falls apart.

When you are firmly grounded in your fundamental mind, you can protect and guide the consciousnesses that make up your body so that they all work together harmoniously. But if nobody's there, then what? Harmful life forms will invade your body and begin to multiply, spreading throughout it. Soon your nice house will be no more. This is a very real problem.

All of these problems are what you've input in the past, now manifesting in the present. To change that, you have to entrust it all, everything you encounter and every feeling that arises, to your foundation. As you entrust these, this act of letting go and entrusting will erase what was previously input. It's just like how, on a cassette tape, new input erases what was previously recorded there.

This is possible because there's the one in charge within you; the captain who can manage the ship is there. The master of the house is present, and can govern the consciousnesses of the many lives within you.

There has to be the one in charge, who can observe what's going on with those consciousnesses, and, when they go off in a harmful direction, can control and restrain them. If there were no such captain, then it would be like parents abandoning young children at home. Or, think of the problems that might ensue if teenagers brought home all their friends, and then left them alone in the house.

Let me give you an analogy. There's a type of toad that will approach a snake and provoke the snake into eating it. In the beginning, the snake tries its best to not eat the toad, but as it keeps getting teased and harassed, it loses its temper and eats the toad. It does this without realizing what is going to happen next, for this is a toad whose eggs will only hatch inside a dead animal. Once swallowed, the toad's poison begins to kill the snake. After the snake dies, the eggs hatch within it, and eventually small toads will crawl out from between the bones of the snake.

The snake actually sensed that it shouldn't eat the toad, but in its anger, the snake lost control and gave in to urges beneath itself. And died as a result.

So, now you probably understand what I mean. This same situation applies to protecting yourself from harmful viruses and bacteria. There are dangerous microbes that are always trying to get into your body, and there are dangerous microbes that are latent within your body.

Like the toad and the snake, these outer microbes approach a healthy body and provoke it so that they can be "swallowed." That's not a perfect description, but it will do. Once absorbed, these viruses, bacteria, and microbes begin to multiply within the body and cause any number of serious illnesses, including even leukemia. Please think about this very carefully.

These microbes end up causing people no end of suffering. They often grow and increase by consuming the body's blood, and the symptoms of this are often first felt in the toes and fingertips.

Do I even need to say what a horrible thing it is for someone to just sit back and let this happen? To not bring forth your owner, the one in charge, to look after your body is like taking this noble manifestation of our true nature and just throwing the whole damn thing away! Don't you know how hard it is to be born as a human being? It's so hard, and yet even after having a human body, we still have so much work to do in order to become a true human being, let alone a Buddha.

If what I'm talking about seems unimportant, if you think that it's just old folk religion, then, I have to say, this is you disregarding your essence. It's like a bean sprout trying to ignore the very seed it's growing out of.

I've never told you to put your faith in a Buddha statue, in myself, or in some place up above the clouds, have I? The only thing I ever tell you to believe in is your own true seed – your own inherent Buddha essence, the Buddha within you – which is guiding you at all times.

If you keep maintaining sincere faith in this, then the time will come when you realize that statues are a reminder of the inner essence that is moving us, guiding us, and helping us grow and evolve towards levels that are, as yet, utterly inconceivable to you. It's this true nature that is capable of taking care of anything, regardless of distance. Above all else, you must know this seed for yourself. Think carefully about what it takes for a seed to sprout and grow. It can't sprout if it has soil but no moisture. Nor can it grow if it has water but no soil.

Where can you find that seed once it's sprouted and grown? It's right here, in the tree before you. Nonetheless, people have a tendency to search for something that looks like the past shape of the seed. But that has already transformed into something different. This is what past *Seon*[11] masters meant when they said, "The past doesn't exist because it's moved on." That seed doesn't exist somewhere else, with some other shape. It has transformed into the tree, which is you, right now.

You are all so impressive to me. You have good educations, lead comfortable lives, and understand how this modern world works. I'm so grateful to every single one of you. Because of you, I've been able to learn so much.

And yet, in this life, even a single blade of grass is our teacher. Even a rock alongside the road is our teacher. So regardless of how long you've practiced, or how much you've studied, don't let yourself

---

11. Seon(禪)(Chan, Zen): Seon describes the unshakeable state where one has firm faith in their inherent foundation, their Buddha-nature, and so returns everything they encounter back to this fundamental mind. It also means letting go of "I," "me," and "mine" throughout one's daily life.

fall into the trap of thinking that there's nothing more for you to learn about Buddhism or spiritual practice.

Further, everything you're seeing and experiencing, everything you think is going well or badly – you're able to experience and think about all of those things because you're here, because you were born into this world. If you didn't exist, how could any of those thoughts, feelings, or interactions have existed? Because you are here, all of this other stuff is possible.

I'm trying my best to use different expressions and help you understand this, but I'm not well educated, so I can't always explain things as well as I'd like. But what else can I do? All I can do is try to explain, using bits and pieces from here and there. Yet ultimately, the terms I use aren't important, they're just a method. You have to do the work to grasp the truth that underlies all of these. I can't tell you how critically important this is.

One of the things I wanted to talk about today is this issue of harmful things – both those coming from outside your body as well as those arising from within it – and how you can handle them and also protect your body, so that you can grow and evolve. When you can see for yourself how these kinds of problems can change the course of a person's life, it's often quite terrifying.

However, most people haven't given the least bit of thought to issues like this. That's why I take every opportunity that I can to tell you how serious this is, and to show you how to take care of these things for yourself. When I see the needless suffering and pain people go through because they don't know this, well, there's a reason my eyes well up with tears several times a day.

The thing is, I can't make others behave in accordance with what I know to be the best way forward. All I can do, all any of us can do, is think of others with kindness and compassion, and help guide them according to their own level of understanding. Do this harmoniously, without looking down upon those still lost in ignorance. Also, in the same vein, don't place those who are doing well on a pedestal.

Take care of things in this way because all the lives within your body are acting upon and following your thoughts. They just mirror your generosity – or your narrow-mindedness. This is why it's often so hard to raise thoughts from our foundation. It's something we have to work hard at.

Some people, well, many people actually, have similar experiences of when they began to make this connection with their foundation. One of the members here put it this way.

"Sunim, I really didn't understand how precious this fundamental mind is when I was home in Korea. But when I went overseas, I felt so lonely and often called to *Juingong*[12] from the bottom of my heart. Especially when something happened to me, or when I couldn't keep up in class, I had nothing. All I could do was call to Juingong – and you – for help. I would call for help and try desperately hard to entrust all of my problems to this fundamental mind. As I kept doing this, I found myself keeping up with my classes."

There was another episode involving this lady. While she was out, a burglar broke into the room she was renting. She had almost nothing, and as the

---

12. Juingong(主人空): Pronounced "ju-in-gong." Juin (主人) means the true doer or the master, and gong (空) means "empty." Thus Juingong is our true nature, our true essence, the master within that is always changing and manifesting, without a fixed form or shape.

Daehaeng Sunim has compared Juingong to the root of the tree. Our bodies and consciousness are like the branches and leaves, but it is the root that is the source of the tree, and it is the root that sustains the visible tree.

burglar searched her room, he found a poem that she'd written, describing how hard life was, being so poor and far away from her home country, and how sad she felt. You can't imagine what happened next: When she came home that evening, she found her poem on her desk, and folded up inside it was a thousand dollars!

Whoever it was that broke into her room was so moved that instead of stealing from her, he gave her money! She wrote about this to me, calling it a miracle, and still in shock that her foundation could work in such a way. Like the saying goes, when you're standing right next to a lighthouse, you don't realize how bright it is until you move away from it. Then you can appreciate just how bright and wonderful that light is.

This same thing applies to you and your own root. This root is so much a part of us that people don't even see it. Your root is so close to you that once your practice has deepened, you can easily communicate back and forth with it. It's just so amazing. Imagine the feeling of connection that comes from always being in touch with your root and always being able to communicate with it!

Yet there are people who get twisted around and start trying to find something more powerful or dramatic outside of themselves. But those who seek like this, chasing things like ki and such, often end up experiencing all kinds of unpleasant side effects. They may hear things that aren't there, feel a horrible pressure in their head, or even levitate off the ground. However, those who seek their root by trying to directly entrust it with the stuff that comes up in their everyday life don't experience any of these harmful things.

Instead, a firm awareness of their own root grows within them, and their spiritual practice becomes more and more deep. They become able to answer their own questions, to see for themselves, to feel for themselves, and to respond fully and completely to whatever arises.

Let me talk about something else now. Until you've awakened, you can't possibly imagine the power this practice has to affect even the functioning of the universe. Through your Buddha-nature, you are connected to the Buddha-nature of everything in the universe. Their energy and our energy, our Buddha-nature, are functioning together as one, just one. That is what I mean when I say that our Buddha-nature is connected to the Buddha-nature of the universe. This energy is so huge and incredible, you just can't imagine it.

Nothing in this universe – not the planets, not the stars – stays still. It is all ceaselessly functioning and performing its own role, and has its own life span. Humans, stars, and bugs all have different life spans and roles, but their Buddha-nature is working together as one. This energy is so magnificent! I desperately wish that people would make spiritual practice something important in their lives, and so awaken to this for themselves.

But when I look around at the world, there are so few people, almost no one, really, trying to connect directly with their own root. It seems like everyone is praying to outside objects. They set up something outside themselves, believe in it, and then beg that for help.

I wish there were more people who realized that their own root is the most important thing of all, and who were focused on how to connect with it and develop this great inner potential.

With this, everyone can take care of any kind of problem they encounter, both things of the visible realm as well as of the unseen realms, and do so with a steady heart.

So, my hope is that you all will practice this diligently and be able to take care of whatever arises. Even words like "practice" and "study" are just labels, terms we use to communicate. The important thing is that you truly practice relying upon and using this root, this connection, so that you can take care of the problems of the Earth, and even of the Universe itself.

If there's a problem with the Earth, its effects are not going to be limited to just our solar system. Because all aspects of the universe are interconnected, their problems likewise affect each other. For example, if our sun reached the end of its life and either burned out or expanded wildly, life in this solar system would be wiped out, of course. But throughout the universe, there are dimensions and many living beings that have a connection with life on Earth, so the harm to life in those places, too, would be terrible beyond imagining.

There's absolutely nothing that remains motionless and unchanging, not on this Earth, not the Earth itself, nor any single thing in the whole universe. All of it is ceaselessly moving, expanding, and contracting. And not just in the visible realm: the unseen realms and the realm of Buddha-nature are all ceaselessly changing, with time and space counting for nothing.

Suppose some huge disaster was about to happen in Korea; how would you take care of it?

What if huge parts of the country were about to sink into the ocean, or high mountains were going to flatten out, or plains were going to rise up to become mountains, or continents were going to merge together or pull apart, causing volcanoes to erupt, and so on? The Earth is constantly changing and moving like this.

How then, can we manage those problems? How can we guide them toward a less harmful outcome? In this interconnected and constantly changing whole, there is no one fixed or "right" way to handle things. Instead, if we firmly ground ourselves in our foundation, our root, then, because we are firmly connected with this whole, the best response for that situation will naturally arise. This, too, is a form of what we call *"Doing without any thought of doing."*[13]

Nothing in all the world is more valuable than this ability to rely upon our root. Here, in the Buddha's *Dharma*,[14] there is no "I can do it" or "I

---

13. Doing without any thought of doing: While this can mean thought and action free of any sense of a separate "me" or "I" that's doing things, it also means letting go of the thought that "I" did something or experienced something, once we become aware of that train of thought.

14. Dharma: This refers to both ultimate truth, and the truth taught by the Buddha.

will do it." When you have the ability to take care of something, you just do it. You respond naturally, entrusting everything to your true nature like the flowing of water, with no "me" or "I did." However, by using their minds unwisely, people often end up creating their own problems. They keep scratching healthy skin, until finally it bleeds.

Take the case of the Sampoong department store disaster;[15] the building collapsed because, during construction, everyone from the contractor to the owners were completely absorbed in outer things and didn't give the least bit of thought to the seed within themselves. They couldn't calmly reflect inwardly, and they ignored their true nature, which was trying to lead them in wise directions. Thus, that disaster happened.

If someone in charge had been a practitioner with faith in their own root, then that collapse wouldn't have happened. Of course, such a person

---

15. Sampoong department store: This was a high-end, luxury department store in southern Seoul that collapsed on June 29, 1995, killing 502 people and injuring 937. Its collapse was due to faulty construction, but the death toll was a result of the owners refusing to close the large basement supermarket, despite cracking and booming sounds being heard on the upper floors. They closed the upper floors, but left the supermarket open to take advantage of the late afternoon rush of people preparing for dinner.

wouldn't have cut corners like that in the first place. Anyway, even if that person wasn't awakened and so couldn't truly perceive what was going on, they would still have been given a message in their dreams, at least.

For example, one of the members here worked for a construction company, and one day had a dream where someone called out, "Hey! Something went wrong on this side of the building! Open up that concrete mold and check it out."

So, the next day he went to that side of the building and carefully examined the main concrete support pillars. They looked okay at first glance, but once he started testing them with a hammer, he realized that the several of the pillars were full of air pockets. If that had been discovered after the upper levels were added, they would have had to tear down half the building and begun again. This would have been a huge disaster for his company, so he was thrilled to have found it early, and amazed at how his true nature let him know about it.

Actually, nothing exists apart from our true nature. People are living here right now because their seed gave rise to a sprout. Yet they rush about, thinking they're cut off from everything else. As if a sprout somehow appeared without a seed or a root?!

What does it mean to be alive? To drink even one sip of water involves millions of beings working and living together. There is no "you" that lives apart from everything else.

This isn't some religious teaching. It's science, medicine, and philosophy. All things are connected to each other. Meditation and the sutras aren't separate, nor are your body and Buddha-nature separate. None of it can be split apart. You can't have a bean sprout without a bean seed. Without the bean seed, the sprout couldn't exist, and without the bean sprout, there could not have been a bean seed.

And yet people say things to me like, "Oh! I'm so busy, I just don't have time to practice," which is just such a ridiculous idea that I can only laugh out loud. Do you know why? Your life itself is nothing other than the process of a seed becoming a sprout, living its life, and then forming a seed again.

I've never told you to go off and meditate for a hundred days or to go do 3,000 bows, have I? If you happen to have some free time, sit down and ask your true nature to show itself, to give you a sign that it exists. If you're busy, then just do this as you work. Practice like this wherever you are, whatever you're doing, whether you're walking, standing, or sitting on the toilet.

Wherever you are, no matter whether that place is dirty or clean, that's where Buddha exists. Right there, all things and life are connected together and communicating as one.

So it's just absurd to think that you don't have time to practice. There are these kinds of uninformed people, and there are also people who find it hard to practice because they've been trained to pray outwardly, to seek truth outside of themselves.

Let me move on for now. Please don't forget that everything you're experiencing with other people is happening because you're involved. You can't have a bean sprout without a bean seed there under the soil. This is particularly true when it comes to your children. You meet because of every kind of reason imaginable. Sometimes parents and children meet each other because of the good karma between them, and sometimes they meet because there is evil karma between them.

But don't worry about any of this. No matter whether your kids fill you with joy, or make you feel like they drove a railroad spike through your heart, yelling at them or even hitting them won't make things any better, will it? It only makes things worse. It just makes your children want to run away from home. [Sighs.] A lot of you have probably suffered through things like this.

[To the audience, who are sitting cross-legged on cushions in the Dharma hall] Go ahead and stretch out your legs. It's completely okay. You're the only one who can take care of your body. Nobody else can, or will, do it for you.[16]

How should you handle these kinds of family problems? Think back to what I just said: you and your root are inseparable. Everything arises, or not, through the functioning and power of this inherent nature.

So entrust everything back within yourself, reminding yourself that, "It's you, true nature, through which karma can arise, and it's you that can keep it from arising. This flesh I have isn't my foundation, and it isn't my true shape. This 'me' doesn't exist at all. So 'I' don't have to get tangled up in these things. It's you, as the whole, that can take care of all this."

And then, deeply entrust where you are now and what you're facing to this essence, and just keep observing.

---

16. In Korean temples, it's considered rather rude to point the soles of your feet at someone. So in Dharma halls, people are reluctant to stretch out their legs in front of them, towards the Buddha statue or a sunim giving a talk.

Even ants have an innate sense of good judgment and can take care of themselves, so how much more so your children? They still need your attention and guidance of course, but you don't need to be too worried about them.

As you probably know, giving children too much can ruin them. They end up not valuing what they've been given, and have no idea how much effort it takes to earn even a little money. And they often end up leading absurd lives. What kind of a future will such children have? So when you give your children an allowance, you shouldn't give them too much or too little. Just keep entrusting everything between you to this fundamental mind of yours, then as your heart becomes brighter, your child's will, too.

Even though as a family you may not be that interested in each other's pursuits, you still love each other, don't you? Share love with them by entrusting the following thought to your foundation, "Your foundation and mine aren't separate. As the light within me becomes brighter, yours will, too." It's this deep foundation that help us brighten our minds and develop a warm, healthy relationship. It's this foundation that can lead you toward wise paths.

Entrusting like this is true love. If you keep doing this, even a child who has run away will do everything they can to return home. This is so true.

Some of you only pay lip service to the idea of Juingong, and then come and tell me things like your son hasn't returned home, or a sick person isn't getting any better. What am I, a doctor? No. It's your own Juingong, your true foundation, that can manifest according to your need, so why wouldn't it manifest itself as doctor?

If you are sick, it will become a doctor for you; if you need to live longer, it will become the spirit of the *Northern Dipper*.[17] If you need a guide in the realm of the dead, it will become *Ksitigarbha Bodhisattva*[18] for you. If you are desperately poor or

---

17. The Northern Dipper: (Also known as the Big Dipper.) Traditionally in Korea, people have believed that the seven stars of the Northern Dipper govern the length of humans' lives.

18. Ksitigarbha Bodhisattva(地藏菩薩): The guardian of the earth who is devoted to saving all beings from suffering, and especially those beings lost in the hell realms.
Bodhisattva(菩薩): A Bodhisattva is traditionally thought of as an awakened being who remains in this realm in order to continue helping those who are suffering. However, in the most basic sense, a Bodhisattva is the manifestation of our inherent, enlightened essence that is working to save beings, and which uses the non-dual wisdom of enlightenment to help them awaken for themselves.

in trouble, it will become *Avalokitesvara*[19] for you. If you are at sea and need help, it will become the dragon spirit in order to help you. It will become the kitchen god, the earth spirit, whatever you need.

So then, what's wrong with you? What's missing? The only thing that was wrong was how you used your mind. So, how you use your mind is completely up to you, as is how you address the things you face. These are there to help you develop; don't cheat yourself by looking for someone else to take care of them. Even if I was somehow able to take care of all the problems facing you, to do so would cause you to lose your potential for growth and salvation. Yet people still bring me these kinds of problems. [Sighs.]

Sometimes, I feel like telling them, "Why do I have to deal with this? This has got nothing to do with me. Why should I have to deal with the results of the things you've done in the past? You made it through your own actions, so take care of it yourself!"

But then I shake this off and remind myself that isn't the right way to think. Those people aren't

---

19. Avalokitesvara Bodhisattva(觀世音菩薩)**:** The Bodhisattva of Compassion, who hears and responds to the cries of the world, and delivers unenlightened beings from suffering.

coming because they think I'm so pretty to look at, they're coming because they're desperate for help.

So, how could I not have compassion for them, how could I not open my heart to them and share their pain? How could I not try to guide them? How could I fulfill my own purpose if I don't have enough compassion to embrace them all as one?

To save just one person may mean hundreds or even thousands of trips to the unseen realm to deal with the causes of the current problems. What finally manifests in the visible realm is the result of vast sweat and toil in this realm of mind. It takes this much hard work to save even a single person.

For example, when someone has a lot of bad karma, it may be that because of their past actions, some other people have fallen into very bad situations or even been reborn as animals. All of this has to be addressed in order to relieve the first person's suffering. To solve any particular problem, there may be a great many connected issues that also need to be solved.

However, until you've deeply awakened and reached the stage where you can do this, there's no need to worry yourself about what you or others might have done in the past. Just work hard at entrusting the things confronting you right now.

Are there any questions? Even if I haven't made myself clear today, please take your wisdom and good judgment and think about what I've said. Set a goal to apply and put into practice what you've heard today.

Questioner 1 (female): Thank you for this opportunity; this is my first time visiting the Seon Center.

My son [indicating the boy next to her] is about to enter high school, but I'm worried because he often feels uneasy and his attention seems to wander. Is there anything I can do to help this?

Kun Sunim: Young man, please listen carefully. Do you suppose that tree [pointing] has any roots, or not?

Boy: I'm sure it does.

Kun Sunim: Yes, although we can't usually see them because they're covered with dirt, right? Well, each human being also has their own unseen root. We call this root by lots of names, such as foundation, true self, or the true doer, but regardless, it's this root that can guide and take care of you.

Within your body there are many, many living beings, and they also have consciousness. They contribute all kinds of thoughts, which can make it harder for you to concentrate. You have to remember that your foundation is the one in charge and the one that can keep those thoughts from running wild.

So, remind yourself that, "It's you, true nature, my root, that can guide me, and it's you that can help me get through school. You're the one that can let me perceive what's really going on, and respond as needed." And entrust it with whatever situation you find yourself in.

This true nature is your root and your source. It's your eternal and best friend, and is never apart from you.

Questioner 2 (female): I really appreciate this chance to meet you and speak to you directly.

I first visited a Buddhist temple about ten years ago, and attended fairly regularly. Then in February of this year, I was given a copy of your book, *Hanmaum Yojeon* (Essentials of One Mind) by a friend.[20] I found it so inspiring, and was amazed

---

20. The core of this book has been published in English as *No River to Cross* (Wisdom Publications, 2007).

that there are still sunims like you in this day and age. Since then my life has overflowed with gratitude.

Before I read that book, I thought Buddhism was something that existed only in Buddhist temples, and wasn't really relevant to my daily life. However, now, the pleasure of the Dharma is always with me in my day-to-day life.

At my job, I've shared your books with my coworkers and several of them have discovered the joy of this spiritual practice. Yet in the case of my own family, I have a hard time sharing it with them. Further, our home is down in Daegu, but my children are going to university in Seoul, so that makes it even harder for me to connect with them.

When they were younger and more willing to listen, I didn't know anything about spiritual practice, and now this is the situation I find myself in. Further, my third daughter is leaving for Italy in a couple of months. Can you give me a method or something so that I can help her understand this Dharma before she leaves?

Kun Sunim: Go ahead and repeat what I just said about a tree and its root. Suggest that before a meal, she simply remind herself of the things she's grateful for, including her family, her root, and so on.

If you teach her like this, then even though it's very simple, that will grow into a great treasure that will bless her so much more than anything like leaving her a large inheritance. It will become a great treasure that will enable her to take care of whatever kind of difficulties she faces in life.

Questioner 2: But my children aren't living with me; they're in Seoul.

Kun Sunim: It doesn't matter. In mind, there is no distance. Suppose that I'm here and there's someone in the US. We can communicate in an instant, regardless of distance, because mind is faster than even the speed of light. This entire planet is no bigger than a room. A room! No matter how many light bulbs are in a room, the same electricity will illuminate them all instantly.

Questioner 2: And this is possible for me?

Kun Sunim: Yes.

Questioner 2: Okay. I'll be sure to teach my daughter what you've said. Thank you.

Kun Sunim: Good. As you keep working at this, you can connect with her, and quietly communicate with her foundation. In this way, her own inner light will become brighter. Also, sending some books and tapes from the Seon Center will help, too.

Questioner 3 (female): It seems the question I have is similar to the previous one. In my case, I have several daughters and a son, but my boy doesn't seem interested in learning about this spiritual practice.

Kun Sunim: In cases like that, the parents need to have first developed their own practice to a certain point, then they will be able to guide their children. I think you'd better guide him by telling him the analogy of the tree and its root, and encouraging him to have faith in the true nature that's always leading him. Once he begins to feel and experience this working in his daily life, he won't lose sight of it.

Questioner 3: I gave him a book published by the Center, called *Maum ui Bulsi* (The Living Spark Within) and although he read it and said he understood it, it didn't seem so to me.

Kun Sunim: Listen, if you want him to know about this, then stop trying to do it through words. Let go of any idea that you know something, or even that you don't know something, and just let the electrical wire that is your mind make contact with the wire that is your son's side. When they connect, energy and light will flow naturally between both sides. This is how to help him know the essence of spiritual practice.

Anyway, it would be better for you to entrust the following, "This true nature, Juingong, will help him find the bright light within himself." If you truly let go and entrust this, then that will be communicated and he'll start to see his own light.

Questioner 3: I understand. Thank you so much for this.

Questioner 4 (female): Hello. I'm a high school senior. Before I saw you today there were a lot of confusing things in my life that I wanted to ask you about. However, as I sat down here today, all of those disappeared, and the only thought that arose within me was that I will walk this path of attaining the Dharma until the end of my life. I can only agree with those sunims who said that this treasure is worth more than anything else in the world.

Lately, I've been feeling very emotional and unstable, and this has made it hard for me to concentrate on anything. When I observe my thoughts, it seems like all kinds of strange things are popping into my mind, flying around within me, and then disappearing, only to be immediately replaced by new ones. I can't quite describe this right; but it fills me with an irrational fear sometimes, and makes me feel suffocated.

Of course, I'm working at entrusting all of this to Juingong, but I was wondering if you had any advice for me.

Kun Sunim: Imagine that you're an infant who can't even walk yet. The only thing a baby needs to do is hold onto the nipple and keep suckling. What is the point of an infant worrying about anything? If it takes a poo, it will be cleaned up. If she needs to sleep, a bed will be provided. The only thing a baby needs to do is feed when she's hungry and sleep when she feels tired. What else is there to worry about?

The only thing you need to do is believe in your root. Completely rely upon it. All those trees [pointing outside] live by relying upon their root. To ask them if they believe in their root is like asking a person if they have a head. Absurd. When you see the leaves and branches, in that instant you automatically know that tree has a root.

You, too, have a root, a foundation that formed you. It's because of this that you were born with this body and are able to perceive everything you encounter and everything in front of you. So, instead of chasing after those things, doesn't it make more sense to rely upon the root that is the source of all that? You are the manifestation of this. Believe in the essence that's formed you, the eternal essence that's the source of your life!

People call it by all kinds of names, but just know that because you're living here now, your Juingong is also here, working together with all the lives in your body, continuously flowing and changing.

Questioner 4: I just attended the summer youth retreat, and experienced something very interesting. There was a mountain hiking program, which was more like a courage test, where we would walk down a trail in the dark as a team.

However my team got lost about halfway down, and strayed quite far into the forest. We'd started at 9 p.m., but it was about 2 a.m. before we finally found our way back to the Seon Center. It even rained quite hard while we were lost.

The whole time, it was clear to me that the only thing I could believe in was Juingong, and I wasn't scared a bit, even though the situation could have turned out quite bad. As I think back on it, the experience feels like a dream.

Kun Sunim: You handled that very well. If you keep going forward like that, you'll be outstanding in whatever you do.

Questioner 4: When we were lost I kept myself focused on Juingong and what you've taught. Even though we were lost and wet, I felt such deep appreciation as we made our way, and now I think that everything that happened was to help me realize how this fundamental mind works.

Kun Sunim: If you've managed to evolve all the way up to a human being, then you have to take advantage of that, and work hard to deepen your spiritual level and seek to realize the truth.

Why? Because only humans, among all the animals, have the unique ability for growth and self-reflection. Many people don't realize that everything in life is an opportunity to practice, so they run around here and there looking for something fascinating, or trying to find some fixed concept they can cling onto.

But the real point of your life is to know who you are. This is what you have to know. When you have faith in your essence, this faith will lead you to who you truly are. When you work at this, when you make an effort towards this, then unseen hands will help and protect you. Even the trees around you will turn into merciful Bodhisattvas that will guide you.

Questioner 4: Thank you so much for this wonderful teaching! I will work hard to realize all this for myself.

Kun Sunim: Good! Words are so inadequate at describing workings of our fundamental mind. It's just so incredible! Now, work hard and experience this for yourself.

Questioner 5 (male): I'm a graduate student, and when my schedule is too busy, I sometimes skip the monthly Dharma talks here, telling myself that I'm too busy or tired. However, after doing this for several months, I began to feel listless, and things in my life weren't turning out well.

So, I started attending the Dharma talks again, even though I was still tired, and I began to feel more connected and positive about everything around me.

My question is this: You've taught us not to rely upon outer things, nor to get caught up in praying to outside powers, and to instead rely upon only our true self. But in my case, I feel like my life goes better when I attend the monthly Dharma talks. If I come to the Dharma talk everything works out better than when I skip the monthly Dharma talks. But lately I've started to worry that all this is just another form of chasing after blessings or good luck.

Kun Sunim: [laughs] How could wanting to go somewhere the Dharma is being taught be begging for something outside yourself? Instead, it is your true essence very straightforwardly revealing itself. What I had meant was to not set up some outer object or power and then pray to it.

Questioner 6 (male): I'd like to ask about something that I think applies to many people. A lot of parents tend to meddle in or try to control their children's lives. Kids often resent this, and their relationship becomes more and more strained and uncomfortable for both the parents and the kids. Is there some method that can completely sweep away these kinds of problems?

Kun Sunim: If you want to completely change your relationships, then you have to completely entrust them. You're the one who has to do it. Will you become full if I eat your breakfast? No.

Our lives are a ceaseless unfolding, a ceaseless flowing and responding. When we're hungry, we go and eat. When there's pressure in our bowels, we find a toilet. And when our body is exhausted, we take a break.

If you strike that bell over there [pointing], it will produce a sound according to your skill at striking it. Those people who decided to come here today will then hear it, and, according to their preferences, will think that it's a good sound or not.

The interactions between parents and children are the same. Your similar karma and levels of spirituality drew you together, and leads to all different kinds of interactions.

You see this with everything in the world. Gold is put together with gold, and iron is gathered together with iron, isn't it? Monks gather with other monks, lay people gather with lay people, politicians spend time with other politicians, and children go and play with other children. Even in grocery stores you see this: apples are placed with apples, and pears with pears.

So, whatever is happening in your own family right now is the result of your own karma and spirituality; it's drawn you together, and it shapes how you respond to each other. If you want to change how things are now, then you have to dissolve the causes that are shaping your circumstances. This is why I keep telling you to entrust all those problems back to your foundation, because that's where they've arisen from, and that's the place that can dissolve them.

I've said this before, but even if your kids ignore their studies, even if they stay out all night, even if they get picked up by the police, don't just yell at them. Don't speak down to them.

Instead, speak with a kind voice. Ask if they've eaten. Ask if they got any sleep. Be tender and kind. If you give advice, do it from the perspective of their well being, "You're the one who's in charge of your life, and the one who needs to take care of it. Please think about your future from time to time."

If you want to be able to help them, your speech has to be gentle – from their viewpoint! If they see your heart as warm and kind, how could they not want to spend more time in such a home. Through mind, you need to create a warm and friendly environment.

When you entrust all of these kinds of problems to your foundation, they become smaller and smaller, and eventually disappear. Parents and children are all connected by this foundation, and when you practice like this, it's like turning on the electricity to a room: in that instant, all the light bulbs in the room become brighter. Parents and children are living in the same room like this.

Because you both already know that you are family, this unseen connection works even stronger. When you entrust your concerns there and speak gently to your child, that entrusting and intention is instantly communicated to your child's fundamental mind. As soon as your light comes on, theirs also becomes bright.

There was a mother and son who had terrible quarrels. They fought all the time and went at each other as if they were enemies. But the mother began to learn this practice of entrusting, and kept at it. One day, her son came home just as she was having a hard time washing the big kimchi pots in their yard. Without his mom saying a word, he just pitched in and helped her move and clean them.

That was the first sign of a transformation that eventually made him seem like a completely different person. It was the result of the communication between them that was occurring because his mother was working at letting go. As her mind became brighter, his did, too.

Because you are inherently connected with others, as you entrust your problems to your essence – your foundation – the light that arises from that entrusting also grows brighter within the other person. So there's no reason to blame others; instead, work on using your mind wisely.

If you can go forward with this kind of wisdom, how could your family not be happy and successful?

Dharma Talk 2

Inherent Connections:
Children, Parents, and the Dharma all around Us

May 5, 1991

This talk was first published in English
as Volume 11 in the ongoing series,
Practice in Daily Life.

Going forward, we all have to develop this practice of relying upon our fundamental mind to the extent that we can take care of whatever confronts us, including even problems of a global scale. We also need to share this practice with others and help them to develop their own inherent ability so that they can use it for themselves. This is something most serious and urgent.

I'm not sure if you're aware of it, but this inherent nature of ours, which is also the fundamental nature of reality, functions without hindrance or limitation. Truly!

Let me give you one, very small example of this: There was an old man who practiced in this temple, and happened to come down with acute blood poisoning. Several doctors all confirmed that he had only a few days to live. I went to his hospital room, and seeing him there, I said, "Let's get rid of all those tubes and needles, and live or die, get out of here." He couldn't speak, but nodded his head weakly. At that moment, because the situation was so desperate, I raised the thought that, no matter what, this man would not be carried off. No matter what!

This fundamental nature functions without hindrance or limitations, so we too need to raise thoughts free of fear, attachments, and limitations! Yet, if we get hung up in ideas such as, "It's too hard," "I can't take anymore," "That's no good," and so on, how can we function as our true nature, working in accord with this great, unhindered reality?

In the early 1960s, when I was helping to rebuild Sangwon Temple (in the Chiak Mountains), I encountered all kinds of difficult situations. To overcome those, I couldn't dwell on reasons or excuses; I just had to approach the situation unconditionally.

If we give rise to a thought from this utterly unhindered, wise, and profound reality that's sometimes given the name *"Buddha-dharma,"* [21] then such a thought functions as one with everything and so can save everything. There is no "big" or "small" in this.

When I make up my mind to do something [she thrusts her fist into the air in a sign of determination], I throw my whole heart into it. Even if the pain coming to me from the situation fills me with tears, I keep my eyes firm and unwavering. We

---

21. Buddha-dharma: In general this refers to the living, breathing, fundamental reality that the teachings of Buddha point towards, but it occasionally means the teachings themselves.

have to raise intentions in this way – fearlessly and free of all discriminations.

If you take Juingong, something that is inherently part of you, and set it up as if it were some kind of deity, praying to it and asking it to take care of this and that, then because you're viewing this part of yourself as something separate, the thoughts you give rise to will have no power to manifest into the world.

Of course, you'll see this for yourself after you awaken. The very act of relying upon your foundation is your Juingong, or "true doer," proving its existence. And, completely entrusting even what I've just said is also relying upon your foundation. When, from deep inside, you feel that something absolutely must be done or resolved, then do it unconditionally. Unconditionally! Just jump straight in!

Similarly, people sometimes get caught up in notions such as cutting off useless thoughts; however, all the different kinds of thoughts that arise aren't just things to be cut off. They are materials for your practice, and the stuff that will make it possible for you to grow up and awaken.

Thus, these "false" or "useless" thoughts aren't something to get rid of – just acknowledge them and move forward. If you're too concerned about these things, then that worry itself becomes a hindrance to you. Those concepts of "false" and "delusive" are just things somebody else made up; don't let yourself be disturbed by them.

Everyone in the world has gone through extremely difficult times to get to where we are now. Wasn't that enough? Do you really want to go on like that forever, always suffering and being swept away by this or that, unaware of the very marrow that makes it possible for you to live?

The essence of this is right before your very eyes. It's in everything you do, and is fundamental to every aspect of your ordinary, daily life. This marrow, this Buddha essence is right there with you, so stop thinking it's somewhere far away. This mysterious functioning is always right in front of us, and is so profound.

Look at the world around us. When a doctor says words like "cancer" or "leukemia," just hearing those words often paralyzes people with fear and causes them to lose all hope. As the disease eats into their bones, in their suffering, they panic and give up. Because they give up, they are given up. To put it another way, the lives in their body give up and the surrounding world abandons them as well. The principle behind this applies to everything. You really need to understand this.

There was a man who heard from the doctors that a disease had spread throughout his bone marrow. They told him that bacteria were eating away the inside of his bones. He received the same diagnosis from six different hospitals. He came to see me, so I looked carefully at him and told him that his bones were actually free of anything serious. Instead, it was just something similar to a cold.

It would have been nice if he had understood this principle, but he didn't know anything about it. So, the first thing I had to do was get him to let go of his fears and put his mind at ease. To begin with, I told him to give rise to the very firm determination that he would never have that disease.

In order to pay for medical treatments and hospital visits, he had already sold his house and lands. By the time he came to see me, he was living in a tiny room at someone else's house. He didn't know anything about this practice, so I had to give him something to hang on to. Ultimately, it's not the particular medicine that cures people: it's the functioning of the Buddha-dharma that enables that medicine to help people. This wondrous Buddha-dharma itself is truly the medicine.

So next, I asked him if he had enough money to buy a small bag of potatoes, and he said that he did. I told him to grate the potatoes and squeeze the juice out of the pulp using a piece of cheesecloth. After letting it settle, he should drink the clear liquid between meals, with some roasted grain powder mixed in. If the taste was too strong, he could add a little brown sugar to sweeten it.

Think about this: does potato juice sound like it should work for such a disease? Yet he had deep faith in what I said, that he would be fine. If he'd had a lot of medical knowledge, he probably wouldn't have had any faith in what I said.

He had seven children, the last born when he was fifty, so you can imagine how desperate his circumstances were once he became ill. Yet thanks to his faith, he is alive today, and is looked after by the son who was born when he was fifty. All of this is possible because of the mysterious and profound nature of the Buddha-dharma. Even after you think you understand it, it continues to surprise you.

Sometimes, when I encounter a critical situation or someone in great need, a great determination arises within me – "No! Absolutely not!" Everything in this visible world begins in the unseen realms. Raising up a firm and absolute "No!

Never!" is like driving a nail into the problem in the unseen realms, so that it can't manifest. [Holding up a clenched fist.] I do this because I feel heartbroken when I see people suffering; it doesn't matter who they are or what they believe. Raising this kind of firm intention takes the energy of the universe and nails the problem in place, so that it can't move in a harmful direction.

If you are able to truly know how things work, then when you raise intentions in this way, you will naturally be fulfilling the role of a Buddha and manifesting the Dharma. Here, there are no words such as "sufficient" or "lacking," "right" or "wrong," "rich" or "poor," "noble" or "lowly." Words, labels, and theories have no place here.

To reach this point, you have to gather together all of your sincerity and keep gathering it into your foundation again and again, as if you were trying to squeeze blood from your own bones. When this ocean of sincerity has been gathered together into a single drop, well, words just can't describe that. Something came up recently that left me so heartbroken that I've wanted to cry for the last three days; but from this ocean, a single harmonious thought arose like an iron pillar and became one with the whole. As that great energy began to burst forth, my eyes became bright and strong.

We are coming to a time when it will be desperately important that you all know how to work through the unseen realms. If practitioners can raise thoughts from their foundation and take care of things harmoniously and non-dualistically, then this world of ours will survive and truly flourish.

Of course, as you practice, you should be careful not to overstep your ability; otherwise, your efforts can end up causing all kinds of negative effects and chaotic situations. If a small bowl tries to hold too much, its contents will overflow and cause countless problems. Similarly, don't try to force timetables onto your practice or attainment.

We need true practitioners who can go forward practicing through mind in this way, which is the true tradition of Seon, and who can help raise the future generations of practitioners that the world is going to need.

Sometimes people complain that I don't quote the sutras or teach from them when talking about spiritual practice and our fundamental mind. But what is there in this world that is not part of Buddha's teachings? Even a single blade of grass has life and communicates mind to mind with everything else, sharing the same life and freely giving and receiving whatever is needed. Everything is just truth itself, so even people of other religions can appreciate what I say.

The last time I was in San Francisco, I gave a Dharma talk at a hotel. A lot of people came, including politicians, conservative religious figures, and leaders from other religions. Afterward, a number of us had dinner together, and during the conversations several of them were amazed that I could answer so many questions without any hesitation. They were likewise impressed at how harmonious my answers were, and how anyone could benefit from them, regardless of their beliefs.

This is the nature of the truth the Buddha spoke about, which is why I bring this experience up, not because I want to boast about something. The profound and sincere essence of the Buddha's teachings is such that when you have attained the *five subtle powers*[22] but are free from attachments to them, you can then freely share and apply this energy that connects everything. When you can step beyond even this stage, then, through mind,

---

22. Five subtle powers(五神通)**:** These are the power to know past and future lives, the power to know others' thoughts and emotions, the power to see anything, the power to hear anything, and the power to go anywhere.

you can manifest in ten million different ways, freely coming and going throughout all realms, and naturally taking care of things as needed.

Let's take a look at the Earth. It, too, functions like this: it's a material, functioning system where living beings are gathered together, and where particles are continuously coming in and going out through many different routes.

That which we call the *Dharma realm*[23] connects everything both on and beyond the Earth. It also performs three major functions that support life on the Earth: it controls what leaves and what enters the Earth; it controls communications both on the Earth and outside of it; and it determines what is necessary and responds accordingly. All three of these functions work together smoothly and harmoniously.

For example, it's the Dharma realm's role of controlling what enters and leaves that makes it possible for the North and South Poles to function. This, in turn, is what makes it possible for us to

---

23. Dharma realm(法界): The level of reality where everything functions as an interpenetrated and connected whole. Daehaeng Kun Sunim said that this can also be called the Dharma Net, and compared it to our circulatory system, which connects and nourishes every single cell in the body.

move by stepping on the Earth. The Earth functions just like humans: when we eat, we absorb what we need and excrete the rest. Likewise, if the North Pole is where energy enters, then the South Pole is where what's left leaves.

In the case of human beings, this same fundamental essence manifests as unseen particles from our mind itself – you could say that it's the manifestation of our Buddha essence working to protect humans in five different ways. Without this protection and the abilities it makes possible, it would be impossible for us to even walk. It's one of these abilities that makes it possible for us, from the place of our Buddha essence, to appropriately regulate what we draw toward us and what pulls on us. For example, even the air around us is filled with microbes, and while some are good for us, there are others that should be kept out, or sent out.

Microbes aren't the only thing that we have the ability to regulate, nor are they the only thing that we must regulate. If in the course of our unfolding *karmic affinity*,[24] genetic problems were to arise, or ghosts were to enter a person, those could make

---

24. Karmic affinity(因緣)**:** The connection or attraction between people or things, due to previous karmic relationships.

someone's life very difficult indeed. For example, if you are pregnant and those sorts of things are allowed to enter without any control or filtering, then they could enter the fetus and cause serious problems. A child who may have previously had the potential to be president of a country may now not be able to lead even small groups.

If humans try to live without learning to apply this Buddha essence, we will end up as slaves to the unseen forces. Should this come to pass, we would have no control over our lives, with each new day bringing only chaos. This is why the Buddha said words to the effect that you already have your foundation and self-awareness, so learn to live freely and be a slave to neither the material realm nor the unseen realms. There's no time to waste. None of us knows what will happen tomorrow.

Which is to say, live firmly centered on your foundation. Then, you can't be dragged this way or that. However, if you aren't centered upon your foundation, you're like an empty house that has no owner – countless beings are able to wander in freely and will end up destroying your house.

When you are fully present as the owner of your own house, I can send my energy and ability to you, and they can become one with yours and do great works. However, if you aren't there in your house, your body, then I can't send anything to you. If there's no owner, your body is like an empty house, and all kinds of beings, including human spirits and animal consciousnesses, can freely enter and leave. Coming and going as they wish, they create all sorts of problems and end up destroying your body. With a broken down and crumbling body, it's hard to even think about spiritual practice, let alone to actually meet your true nature.

The Buddha, too, told people not to follow ascetic practices that just end up destroying the body. Instead, he taught that we should practice through mind. He wanted us to know that which is really doing all things. He also said that although our body returns to its basic elements, this true mind of ours endlessly saves us; it saves the lives that make up our body, as well as countless beings outside our body.

Sakyamuni taught that even though millions of beings awaken, they are all still just one Buddha, right here. The great feet of Buddha have already reached every corner of the universe. In other words, even though millions of beings have awakened, your true mind is right here, functioning as one with everything, and it's this true mind that can save you, as well as the land you live in. And when you can transcend time and space and become one with the awakened ones, the fragrance of your true mind will spread throughout the world and function in all manner of ways. Isn't this a wonderful teaching?

The Buddha taught this same idea in the *Diamond Sutra*, the *Flower Garland Sutra*, and the *Heart Sutra*. Even though the idea wasn't expressed this explicitly, it's still there, written very clearly in words that are not words.

A few days ago, a visiting Buddhist monk said to me, "The *Heart Sutra*, just as it is, has an incredibly profound power to it. Why is your temple using a modern, Hangeul translation instead of the traditional version?" What he meant was that the Buddha's teachings, as written down so long ago, should be chanted without any modifications.

So, I gave him the example of what we used to call an "A-frame porter." These were the guys who used an A-frame pack to carry and deliver stuff. When someone needed help moving something they would send for a porter, but nowadays people use a truck or a moving service.

If you were to go around shouting for a porter, nobody would respond, would they? Because they're not "porters," they're "movers" or "moving companies." When I said this, the monk laughed, and said he was grateful there was someone who had the ability to truly translate the sutras.

I've been talking about a lot of different things today, but don't misunderstand my intention. I'm not trying to awe you or imply that you should follow me. Rather, I mean that the truth, the middle path that the Buddha taught, is so profound and great. If you would follow anything, follow that.

Now, let's see if there are any questions.

Questioner 1 (male): I'd like to ask you about *habits*.[25] In the past, you've said that our mind is constantly changing and flowing, so fundamentally there's no place for habits to stick to, nor is there even any place for karma to attach. Yet even though this is so, somehow, for eons, unenlightened beings have created habits and then been caught up in those habits, going through untold suffering because of them.

---

25. Habits(習)**:** These include not just the ways of thought and behavior learned in this life, but also all of those tendencies of thought and behavior that have accumulated over endless eons.

Having carried around these habits that are causing us so much pain for so long, how can we ever be free from them?

Kun Sunim: It's fairly straightforward. First, you need to entrust everything that arises back to your foundation, along with the very firm thought, "Okay, true self, you need to prove that you exist!"

Second, deeply trust your inherent foundation, and know that it has the power to truly take care of what's going on in your life and family. So entrust all of that stuff there, and let it work! It's your true nature that's doing everything, so why do you need to feel so choked and burdened? Leave behind all ideas about whether things went well or not. Whether something is frustrating, going badly, or going well, it's all being done by that essence.

But you can't stop at the point where you only know this fact. As I said earlier, absolutely everything arises from your foundation. So, if you can entrust everything to your foundation, if you go straight in, if you are fierce in your determination to let go of attachments to "I," even in the face of fears about your own death or your family members, then nothing else will bother you or be that difficult. Why do you need to feel so suffocated when all the

Buddhas in the universe can become one with you? It's your greed and desire that makes you feel like that.

Even though you don't give rise to ambitions, you can still wisely take care of everything you encounter with your head held high. If you have to use a sword, then pull it from its sheath without hesitation and hold it high. Of course, if you draw your sword with an evil mind, then it can kill people; but if you draw it forth to save people, then it can save countless people and even build a country.

There's no need for things to be so difficult. What's the big deal if we die today instead of tomorrow, or if even our whole family dies? Does what I am saying seem too severe? [Sighs.] We're just passing through this world. We just walk forward in life doing our best with what confronts us. Still, you need to realize why you're here and what you have to do with your life. When you understand this, it will be like a great weight has been lifted from you.

View your stay in this world like just a brief camping trip, thinking, "Even though I'm out here, the Dharma realm knows everything I feel and experience. It's always looking after me, so what do I have to worry about?" If you go forward with this attitude, then truly, you won't have much to worry about. Even if the entire world were about to be destroyed, you wouldn't be worried about anything. When your mind is this settled, you can actually save the world.

But how could you do this if every little thing rattles and worries you? All of this is true for family problems as well. Frankly, there aren't really any alternatives: we have to either become someone like this, or we will be swept away.

Once there was a sunim who only half-jokingly asked me to nail shut the door of the tiny hut he was staying at. He said he would go in, and then I would nail the door shut behind him. I asked him why he wanted me to do this; he answered that if he couldn't leave the hut, there would be only two choices: awaken or die.

If you understand the principle I was just talking about, you can go through life with a relaxed, generous heart. As you go forward one with all, you breathe life into everything you encounter, and smile so much that people think you're nuts.

Even if you see a bunch of cows on their way to the slaughterhouse, you can smile without any fears for them. You don't have any pity at all for them because, through mind, you can immediately become one with the cows' minds and save them instantly. Even though ten thousand cows died, if you can save them like this, then it's as if you're gathering individual raindrops and helping them flow to the sea. And when those raindrops meet the sea, they are all just one. There is only the water of the ocean. This is so marvelous.

Our minds function as one through the foundation, so this is called "one mind." The ability of this one mind is so powerful that sometimes it's called "Immeasurably Vast Mind," and sometimes it's just called "the Profound Dharma." If there's someone who feels pity for cows on the way to the slaughterhouse but who then tries to help them by going and chanting at the temple, well, I can only say that they don't understand this principle. You need to be able to save them all right now. If someone understood this principle of one mind, they wouldn't wait until later.

So, if you truly awaken and understand this principle, then you save beings in the same instant that you become aware of their need. Whether it's ten cows or ten thousand, when you entrust them all to your foundation, they become one with you. One mind. And becoming one with you like this helps them a great deal in evolving into human beings.

Furthermore, those who have evolved through one mind, when they are finally born as humans, will be people of high quality. Such people would be great beings – resourceful, full of tolerance and wisdom, and able to help take care of the world. We all have this potential, so don't allow yourself to live a narrow, miserable life. If you're always caught up in small things, the influence of that will also make it hard for your children to live up to their potential.

Questioner 1: When I hear your teachings like this, I feel like I'm about to awaken and fly into the sky like a bird.

Kun Sunim: Look! Don't try to awaken! [Laughs.] If you're focused on something called "awakening," you'll wind up filled with frustration.

Take yourself as you are, and in each stage of your practice, just keep going forward on the path in front of you, taking things as they come. Be focused, calm, and centered on your foundation. And when something serious hits you, hit back with, "Hey! Let's take care of this!" From that instant on, it will begin to change.

Of course, it usually takes some time for the results to work their way into the material realm.

But as you entrust things in this way, then, like a blast furnace heating up, there will be cases where your foundation instantly melts down what you've entrusted, and immediately sends it back into the world with a new shape. But how could someone experience this if they aren't relentless about entrusting the situations and emotions that confront them?

Everyone is just passing through this world for a short time – just visiting and then leaving – so don't waste your energy chasing riches, fame, or even health. And don't use this practice to chase after those. When you do encounter something very serious or dangerous, firmly raise the thought, "No! It should go like this!" This method really works. When I realized that incredibly serious situations were developing, I would shout "No!" and slam my fist on the table. A mind like this becomes deep waters, thus large boats can sail there and take many beings across.

Thus, for the sake of our practice, let's always try to leave time for discussion and questions when we have these first Sunday Dharma talks. And through our practice, let's heal our wounds and lead all the beings within us to enlightenment. Then those awakened beings within us will constantly leave our body and return, functioning as a billion manifestations of Buddha nature as they work for the well-being of yourself, others, society, and for the harmony of the world.

In order to be able to bring harmony to the world and save others, we have to take care of our house, the Earth. Taking care of this house called the Earth is one of our duties, and taking care of the home that is our body is another of our duties. You've received your bones and flesh from your parents, so it's your duty to take good care of those and do your best to become a true human being.

Even though you're born with a human body, if you aren't trying to become a true person, how could you say that you've honored your parents? Being a good son or daughter doesn't mean just being respectful and taking care of your parents. Leading a good life and becoming a true person is the way to truly repay your parents.

I didn't realize that today was Children's Day until just before the talk. I said to the sunims here that we should prepare some snacks or something, because a lot of kids would undoubtedly come with their parents today. But the sunims were a step ahead of me, and had already prepared all kinds of Children's Day treats. They're so wonderful!

Okay, let's talk a little more about what it means to be a good daughter or son. When children are sick or hurt, parents feel terrible, don't they? Nothing's fun anymore, and laughter disappears from your life. No one truly realizes what parents go through until they themselves become a parent.

So don't be stupid with your body. When young people are overflowing with energy and do things that damage their body, it often becomes hard for them to be of help to their parents or their country.

There is a well-known Buddhist teaching that says we should practice and attain enlightenment, and save all those lost in ignorance. But, when your body is breaking down and being destroyed, it's so very hard to even practice, let alone awaken and be able to save the beings within your body. Further, if you can't help those beings, then this house of yours will fall into disrepair even faster. If you can't help them evolve, then they can't help you evolve, and if this continues, it becomes a vicious cycle where any evolution is very, very difficult.

Then how do we need to spend our time? People think that there are things like the past, present, and future, don't they? Yet in reality, the past, present, and future are all one, and functioning as the energy that connects everything. They are all inherently functioning and flowing like this, so if you are not caught by life and death, and are free from attachments and fears about those, then you can live in accord with this eternal moment where the past, present, and future are all one.

A couple of weeks ago, our office manager asked me for the short, one page Dharma talk that will be read out during the Buddha's Birthday celebrations. I was a bit surprised, because Buddha's Birthday was still a month away. But he said that they needed it early in order to send it out to all of our overseas branches. This made sense, so I told him to write down what I was about to say, then I spoke. I just spoke from deep inside, without really being aware of what I was saying.

After he finished writing, I asked him to read it back to me. As I listened, I saw that the talk nicely explained the functioning of the truth in three stages. That Dharma talk was something I was doing for the future, which I was taking care of in the present, and as soon as I spoke, those words were in the past. I'd already let go of it and moved with the present moment. The past, present, and future are a flowing whole like this, so every instant is the moment Buddha appeared in the world.

This means that the Buddha exists right here, where you are now. You can see this even in the date of the Buddha's birthday. It's April 8th, right? [On the Korean lunar calendar] April is the fourth month, and the number "4" means East, West, South, and North, i.e., every direction, every piece. When we add another "4" to this to include all of the "directions" of the unseen realms, then "8" symbolizes everything throughout all visible and invisible realms. So April 8th means everything throughout all realms working together and transcending time and space.

Isn't this a wonderful meaning? It means that the Buddha is here in this very moment. He never left, nor did he come from somewhere else. This very moment where you are is the eternal moment of the Buddha appearing in the world. Please engrave this deeply within your heart.

So what do you think now about the meaning of the Buddha's Birthday? Although imperfect, I did a pretty good job with this, didn't I! [Laughs.] In truth, I am imperfect, you are imperfect, and the Buddha is imperfect. Even though he was imperfect, he still awakened to the truth, and later in front of the assembly of monks, he moved over and asked

Kasyapa[26] to sit beside him. How wonderful! He was showing us that we are all inherently one, that we all share the same supreme, perfect place.

In order to teach people this wonderful, supreme meaning, he shared his seat with Kasyapa. Unfortunately, people often just glance at these kinds of stories without deeply reflecting on them. They've heard many similar stories, but it's not easy to understand the deep meaning those stories carry, nor to put that meaning into action.

Does anyone have any further questions? Please ask if you do, and let's not worry about the talk running long today.

Questioner 2 (male): When you teach us, you often say to let go of everything unconditionally and entrust it to our foundation. Yet I found myself wondering who is doing the letting go and who is receiving, and I have come to the conclusion that both are myself. It seems like I'm doing both, so there should be no need to let go, because

---

26. **Kasyapa, or Maha Kasyapa:** Regarded as the foremost of the ten great disciples of the Buddha. He was well known for his self discipline, and the Buddha himself praised Kasyapa for his attainment and realization. After the Buddha's passing, Kasyapa was chosen to lead the great council that gathered to record the teachings of the Buddha.

everything is already right here, but you still teach us to let go. What am I missing?

Kun Sunim: When you make red bean porridge, you have to boil it, so thick bubbles continually arise. Big bubbles, small ones, single ones, and groups of bubbles all come out one after another, just like the thoughts and emotions that continuously arise within us. Anyway, bubbles of all kinds arise within that porridge, yet all of those arise from the porridge and are porridge, so just let them return back to the porridge.

What I'm saying is return it all to the place it comes from. If the bubbles in the porridge were all one size and always arose in the middle of the pot, they wouldn't be a big deal. But sometimes they arise at the edges, and sometimes they're huge, so if they burst on their own, before the cook pokes them, they spray hot porridge everywhere and cause problems. Thus, the story of the *sunim*[27] who was cooking porridge: as bubbles formed, she

---

27. Sunim: Sunim is the respectful title for a Buddhist nun or monk in Korea.

would poke them with a spoon, saying, "You are *Manjushri*,[28] and you, and you, too!"

In the course of our day-to-day life, all kinds of concerns and worries arise. We find ourselves worrying about our health, money, problems at work, being criticized by our boss, our kids behaving badly, fights with our husband or wife, and just every kind of thing. Yet all of those are just bubbles in the porridge. They are porridge, and they all arise within the same pot, so return them all back to this place they're arising from. Have faith that the place they arose from is also the very place that can resolve them.

No matter what kind of situations or feelings arise, they still come from your foundation, so just return them there and don't let yourself fall into worries. Even if your child storms out, saying they're going to kill themselves, don't give in to worry. Remind yourself, "Even this arises from my foundation," and entrust it all there. If you can do this, your child won't behave in a harmful manner.

---

28. Manjushri: The Bodhisattva who represents the essence of wisdom. Manjushri is traditionally portrayed holding the sword of wisdom in his right hand, and in his left hand holds a blue lotus that represents the flowering of wisdom, while riding a lion that represents courage and majesty.

Why is this? We are all inherently connected, so when you entrust a thought to your foundation, it is automatically communicated to everyone and everything. It's communicated to the whole, but is often felt the strongest by those closest to us: our brothers, sisters, parents and children.

For example, when you feel that something is urgent, or feel affectionate, they can sense that. So when you entrust a thought to your foundation, in that instant, it's communicated to your family. It really happens like this. The thoughts you raise really are communicated to them.

So if your child runs away, raise warm, caring thoughts for them, and sooner or later, your child will want to come back home. The thoughts you entrust are sent to them automatically. You don't exist apart from each other; both of you are together within one mind. How could they not respond to your concerns?

Suppose your child really wants to do something that, to you as an adult, seems totally unreasonable. You should still be open to it, saying, "Okay, if you really want to do that, go ahead. I'll support you." At the same time, you should firmly entrust the thought that it turns into a useful experience for them and others, but that having experienced it, the child will soon lose interest in it.

Then, because this communications network exists between you two, after your child tries that thing, they'll find it wasn't as interesting as they supposed. "Dad, I want to quit that now." "Oh, why?" "You know, it's just okay." And often they'll find something else that interests them more. This is the way to raise your family – communicating directly, through mind, with love, generosity, and trust. This is truly loving someone.

However, when children screw up, parents often just start with the yelling, "Where the hell did you go last night? You were supposed to be studying! Do you know how hard your father works to support you?!" As if kids never notice things like that! [Audience laughs.]

Instead of just leaping to assumptions and making accusations, "You couldn't call?!" "How could you...?!" it would be better to actually listen to the child's explanation. After listening to what your child has to say, if it turns out they really did screw up, then try to suggest something positive that they can do if they find themselves in a similar situation. "Honey, in that case, what about trying...?" while entrusting that situation to your foundation.

If, on the other hand, it turns out that your child had a good reason, then encourage them. For example, if their friend had some family emergency, "Actually, I think that was a great thing to do. What kind of place would this world be if we didn't take care of each other?" With positive encouragement like this, it's very unlikely that children will lose their way or fall into dark paths.

A child's education actually consists of three parts. The first is what they learn from their parents. The second part is what they learn from their teachers at school. And the third part is what they themselves learn from trying to manage their own thoughts and behavior as they go forward in the world.

When all three parts are going well, children are generally respectful and civil towards their parents. When they have to bring up a difficult subject, they're polite about it, and when talking about something funny or interesting, they don't use foul or rough language. And in general they tend to enjoy talking with their parents, because they respect, esteem, and love them.

The world is moving so fast these days that kids who are only twenty years old are as mature as thirty-year olds used to be. Society is changing this quickly, so parents need to think that much more deeply about how to raise their children.

When raising children, you have to pay attention to all kinds of small things, don't you? If you can't be there when your child returns home, leave some kind words to let them know you care about them. "Honey, I made you some dinner and left it in the fridge. Go ahead and warm it up. I don't know when you'll be coming home, but I hope you don't get too tired or hungry. I love you!" Be caring and centered, but don't let yourself fall into anxiety.

Try to leave your children short messages like this. When they see these, they can't help but be aware of your love and concern, even if they give no outward sign of having noticed it. Kids who grow up in this kind of warmth and love will naturally feel close to their parents, even in their old age. This is exactly how it happens.

The reason I bring this up is because whether you live in Korea or some other country, raising kids isn't easy these days. Society has become so complex. Moreover, in some places parents have to worry a lot about drugs, don't they?

Are there any more questions?

Questioner 3 (female): I went to Germany in 1971, and have worked there as a nurse ever since. I'm returning in a few days, but would like to ask you about something. My father has passed away, but my mother is still alive. This coming Wednesday is Parents' Day, and while I would like to be a good daughter, I have so much hatred towards my mother.

I had to leave for Germany when I was twenty-five. Even before that, for the first twenty years of my life I suffered so much, I can't even describe it. Even though I excelled in school, I couldn't go to college. Unlike others, I didn't even want to go to Germany, but had to because our family was so poor and needed the money. And for similar reasons, I also never had a chance to marry.

For years I had so much anger and resentment towards my mother about all of this. Now, though, I just don't feel anything towards her. I have no love for her. She's nothing to me. I guess it's because I suffered so much, but I just can't laugh or cry about things the way normal people do. I'm not quite sure how to explain this; I've lived in Germany for so long, it's hard to fully express myself in Korean.

Kun Sunim, how can I heal this illness of my mind?

Kun Sunim: I understand. While your own hardships may have felt unimaginably severe, my own were actually much worse, believe it or not. Yet I am so grateful and thankful to my parents. You said that you've felt many things towards your mother, such as extreme hatred, and now extreme indifference, right? However, those feelings, and everything else, exist because you appeared in the world and because your mother gave birth to you. Nor could you have gone to Germany, which although difficult, has also given you good things, hasn't it?

Your mother's existence is what made it possible for you to be born into the world, and because of this, you're able to learn and grow, and also able to learn about your true essence. Because of your suffering you've been able to learn a lot about life and yourself. Without those experiences you would not be nearly as aware of others' pain, love, and resentments. But now you've become a person who can feel deep empathy for others. Your mother indirectly caused you to learn much more than people who grow up in a sheltered environment. In a sense it's like how lions raise their young, by pushing them down hills and river banks so that they learn to claw and fight their way back up.

So just be grateful to your mother, and buy her some nice flowers for Parents' Day. Regardless of how you feel about her, she's still your mother. In Korea, we say that your mother gave you your flesh, and your father gave you your bones, don't we? Your spirit joined with those and became one, and you were born. So be grateful to your parents, throw away all of your resentments, and just say "thank you" to your mother.

It's time for you to walk away from judgments of who did what bad thing. Utterly leave those behind. Drop all of those into the great furnace within you. Turn those thoughts and feeling over to that place; then those things will be melted down and return to the world as something wonderful that can give light to everyone. And your face will shine as well.

Give her the flowers and tell her, "These are the flowers of my gratitude. Please be healthy and live a long time, and I'll try to be a good daughter." You have to let go of your bad feelings towards her. No matter how much she made you suffer, don't give into hatred or resentment. As much as you suffered at the time, your mother was probably going through much worse. Her own suffering was actually many times worse than your own. You need to know this.

It was the extreme poverty of those times that caused both of you to suffer. So, who was responsible for that environment? You both were. How you lived in the past created the conditions that you experienced in this life. So, there's no point in blaming anyone else. You're fed up with suffering like this, right? So now it's time to make a change in your way of thinking.

Questioner 3: Thank you! I understand.

Kun Sunim: [As the next questioner was bowing three times] When you don't have enough time for three bows, just do one bow.

Questioner 4 (female): I really want to sincerely practice and awaken, but I'm wondering if it's necessary for me to leave home and become a sunim in order to do so.

Kun Sunim: Hmm. I'm reluctant to say too much because in general this is the kind of thing that people need to decide for themselves, without interference. Off the top of my head though, a couple of things occur to me.

For example, if someone becomes a sunim and practices, then other people who see your gray clothes and shaved head may be inspired to practice themselves, and may come to learn from you.

Ultimately, anyone with a sincere mind and determination can study and awaken to the truth. It doesn't matter if they are laypeople or not. Lay practitioners who fully awaken can do anything that's needed in the unseen realms.

However, in the ordinary, visible world, it's hard for them to teach large numbers of people how to practice through this fundamental mind.

It's up to you. You're free to decide to become a sunim or not. Practice doesn't depend upon someone being a sunim or not. I'm being perfectly frank, here. If someone becomes a sunim and never learns about their fundamental mind, then what was the point? Even though a thousand people become sunims, if they don't know anything about this essence, then what does it matter? But a sunim who is determined to know for themselves this truth that encompasses all things is far from an ordinary person. Actually, if someone wanted to live an ordinary life, they wouldn't be thinking like this in the first place. [Laughs.]

Anyway, you could hardly call someone ordinary who leaves their family and everything else behind. To be determined to know and apply this truth that's neither black nor white is certainly not an ordinary thing.

That said, no matter what you do in life or what you study, you still need to understand how this fundamental essence that we all have works. For example, if you work in a medical field, you'll need to know this in order to fully treat your patients. Even if you're a scholar, you'll need to know this as well.

If you haven't experienced and practiced using your fundamental nature – your Buddha essence, your true shape – then you will neither recognize nor be able to take care of the fifty percent of reality that arises from the unseen realms. So, however you choose to live your life, it's proper and natural that you should understand this fundamental nature and be able to work through it.

Questioner 4: My only real concern is whether I can follow the unmarried life of a sunim. This is the part I'm doubting myself about.

Kun Sunim: Well, it sounds like you're better off waiting until it's clear to you what you want to do. If someone is constantly pulled back and forth by thoughts of marriage and desire, then it's unlikely they'll be able to fully devote themselves to practice. Then why bother becoming a sunim?

On the other hand, if someone truly understands and applies this practice of relying upon our fundamental mind, they can take care of their family and rescue all beings. They can do this and take care of the entire world, without moving from where they are now. All of this is done through mind, regardless of whether someone is a sunim or not.

This is what true sunims do. They work at becoming one with whomever they encounter. They become one with them. When sunims realize that someone is caught up in a serious situation, they take everything, and with a firm resolution, return it all to their foundation, where it becomes one and flows as one. This is how we can help not only humans, but also ghosts, animals, and every other kind of being to become unstuck and move forward. This is possible because we are all inherently one, not two.

So if you want to be a sunim, become a true sunim who can go forth resolutely, spreading awareness of how to rely upon our fundamental mind. Experiencing this true root of ours, this essence of our life, and sharing it with others is the meaning of "Buddhism." If you would be able to help free even dead people and plants, then become a sunim.

People busy with family life are often so caught up in trying to take care of their families that they don't have much time or energy to think about those things. This is the only real difference between sunims and lay people.

Thank you all for this wonderful day of sharing and laughing!

Finding A Way Forward:
A Gift for Mothers and Children

March 4, 2001

This talk was first published in English
as Volume 12 in the ongoing series,
Practice in Daily Life.

Sitting here together with you, I'm reminded of a funny thing I saw a long time ago. One day, I saw a chipmunk digging in a small patch of sweet potatoes and stealing them. When I first saw him, it was obvious he was trying to dig up the sweet potatoes, but I was curious what he would do once he got one. So I sat there and watched him.

He would dig up a sweet potato, push it onto a flat rock at the edge of the patch, and using that as a platform, he would grab the sides of the sweet potato, put his forehead on it, and then, pushing with his head, would run away carrying the sweet potato on his head. It was so fun to watch!

The reason I mention this story is because there isn't a huge difference between the animal world and the human world. I think a chipmunk that can figure out how to carry away sweet potatoes is much more impressive than a human being who just sits in the middle of his problems without trying to figure out how to wisely overcome them.

Animals and people have different appearances, but the essentials of how we go about our lives are the same. Even though Buddhas, enlightenment, and wisdom fill the air, if you weren't here, trying to find them and become a fully developed human being, it would be as if they didn't exist at all.

After you've been born into this world, and begun to practice with the utmost diligence, you can realize that Buddhas inherently fill the air around us. So don't look for Buddha somewhere far away from you; Buddha is always right where you are. I hope that you all will come to deeply know this for yourselves.

Just because you exist, you'll encounter all kinds of things, but how you react to them determines what happens next. Even in our own family, we sometimes blame and resent each other. We're convinced that everything is someone else's fault, and that we're the victims of it all.

However, when you examine things closely, you'll find that you played a role in all of it. At a very fundamental level, just because you exist, you are feeling and going through those things. There's no use blaming others; it's all something you had a hand in.

If you can thoroughly understand this, then you can take care of everything through mind, instead of trying to solve things by dragging your body around here and there. At this point, it won't be necessary to be reborn with a body.

In fact, look at the way we're already living. Everything we do, see, and hear passes by in an instant. It unfolds naturally, without us trying to control it or let it go. It just flows and changes naturally. This is why it's said that everything is empty.

Please take some time to seriously reflect upon this. If you can flow like this, taking care of things wisely while letting go of thoughts along the lines of "I did" or "This (thing) happened to me," then the pain and hardships of your life will also naturally flow away. Once we let go of "I," there's no place for any of those things to remain.

I've told you to entrust everything to your foundation, Juingong, because, frankly, life becomes plodding drudgery when you're always worrying about having to do this or that, hating others, resenting them, or trying to think your way through every situation. Is this really the best we can do? No! While sitting here taking care of everything, you should also be able to laugh and go for a walk on that mountain in the far distance.

Let me give you an example. This story may seem a bit strange, but bear with me. A man who had awakened needed surgery on his leg, and this was expected to be quite painful. So, when the time came, he left his body behind in the operating room and went to relax in the mountains. After a while he noticed that someone was touching him and trying to wake him up. So he returned to his body, and the surgery was already finished. In this way, he avoided the severe pain of the surgery.

This story may seem kind of hard to accept if you haven't experienced this for yourself, but I'm telling you about this for a reason. As your practice of letting go and relying upon your foundation becomes deeper, you will go through innumerable strange and weird experiences. It's not remotely possible for me to describe them all. How could a few words grasp this flowing that is life? If you're walking along and you find something blocking your way, you move it or go around. You just do this and continue on.

I've told you that when you unconditionally entrust something to your foundation, it responds to that because everything shares the same fundamental connection. It's this response that's sometimes called "Bodhisattva." But this "Bodhisattva" functions according to the needs of the whole, and ordinary people are unable to see the overall picture.

So when you're dealing with all the ordinary, little things of daily life, it's best to let go of your opinions about how they should go, and just unconditionally entrust that situation. Do this, and let go of any stray thoughts of "me" or "I did."

Take it all, whether it's pleasant or unpleasant, going well or not, and entrust it there. Just go forward like this, doing your best to take care of things as they arise. If it seems like you're surrounded by filthy water, or even clean water, don't fall into blame or resentment. Just entrust it all to your foundation. Then it can change into water that's useful to you.

It's not always so easy to grasp the point I'm trying to make. Take the example of a pot of boiling water. Even though I tell you it's hot, at first those are just words; it's difficult to comprehend what "hot" really means. However, after you pour a cup of water, hold the cup, sniff the water, and finally taste it, then you understand.

In order to understand this formless, fundamental essence that we are, we gather here on the first Sunday of every month. As we talk about this, ask questions, and share our experiences, this will help others understand practice and move forward. Some people understand deeply right away, and in others it bubbles and percolates for a while before understanding begins to dawn. In this way, you can develop the ability to truly understand what's going on. Wouldn't that be wonderful? So if you have a question today, please go ahead and ask.

Questioner 1 (male): Thank you for this opportunity! I've heard it said that it's difficult to be born with a human body, to meet the Dharma, and still more difficult to practice and awaken. As an obstetrician, I find myself often thinking about the first of these, and would like to ask you several questions about pregnancy and childbirth.

During the nine months of pregnancy, there can be a lot of problems. First of all, 15% of women experience a miscarriage. In these cases, we believe that something like 60-70% of them are due to birth defects with the baby, and most of these are chromosomal aberrations. We don't know why these happen, and there's nothing we can do to treat them. A certain percentage of miscarriages also occur due to biological issues with the mothers.

That 15% of all women should experience a miscarriage seems like quite a large number to me. If it's possible, could you tell me why these happen? What is the significance of these in terms of the Dharma, and how can I do a better job of treating expectant mothers?

Kun Sunim: Many people have come to me with similar problems. The first thing I tell them is to sincerely rely upon their foundation and entrust it with the problem. However, there's more to it than simply letting go: the parents also have to connect and communicate with the fetus's foundation. This reliance upon our foundation, Juingong, has to be more than just words – it has to move beyond just what we can see and touch.

Let me give you an example. Even though a fetus has spent its life in its mother's womb, it still carries with it all the baggage of its past lives. Sometimes this influence can cause a miscarriage; if a mother feels something like this, she should speak directly to the baby's foundation: "You made this baby, so you should ensure that the child is born healthy." In this way, parents can guide the baby's foundation to help take care of its body.

Let me give you another example. Sometimes the placenta ends up too far down the side of the uterus. In this case, the baby might be uncomfortable enough that it changes position and accidentally wraps the umbilical cord around its neck, or gets it in its mouth. So, it's good to keep relying upon your foundation. The directions you input to your foundation are communicated to the baby's foundation, which then works to take care of the child.

Questioner 1: Thank you. The next thing I'd like to ask you about is morning sickness. Most women experience this to some extent, but for some women, it's quite serious. For some, it's so severe that they choose to have an abortion. We don't know why women have morning sickness, nor how to truly cure it. Could you please talk about this?

Kun Sunim: That's not a difficult problem. If all the things that make up the fetus and mother– their essence, cells, hormones, and so on – can connect with and accept each other, then there will be no more morning sickness.

Even a problem like this turns out to be easy once you understand how to solve it. When a mother communicates to her baby's foundation what needs to be done, then that will begin working to make it happen. In fact, there are also three places on a mother's body that can be used to treat morning sickness: the top of her head, the spine, and the left leg. But, these are all somewhat dangerous if you don't truly know what you're doing, and can lead to bad side effects, such as the mother being left unable to speak.

Questioner 1: The next question I'd like to ask you is about premature birth. Statistically, 11% of pregnant women give birth before the 36th week of pregnancy, and 7% of women give birth before the 35th week. Of children born before the 35th week, 15% don't survive, and many of the rest suffer effects that follow them for the rest of their lives.

Another problem seems to also be that women born prematurely are themselves more likely to give birth to premature babies and to have more problems during the birth. Thus, preventing premature birth is quite an important issue. Is there anything we can do to prevent this or to delay the onset of labor?

Kun Sunim: Even if there was some method like that, it wouldn't be fully effective. Just to give you a very limited, simple example, it's almost impossible for doctors to successfully go in with their hands and correct something with the baby, right? This is why I'm always telling parents to work on communicating with the fetus. If they can truly connect with it, then that problem will immediately start dissolving. Truly. There are so many variables that it's not possible for me to go into all of the reasons why a mother might give birth prematurely.

In general though, many times it's because there are three parts of a mother's body that need to be working together harmoniously, but which aren't. If these are out of balance, the placenta will be damaged, and in some cases it will even begin to separate from the uterus.

Questioner 1: As you say, what we call placental abruption, where the placenta partially peels away from the wall of the uterus, is considered to be the most common cause of premature birth.

Kun Sunim: When, through her foundation, a mother communicates with her unborn child, the child's body can't perceive that, but its own essence, its foundation, hears what the mother is saying. That baby is a being who has evolved through millions of years and who has a great desire and ability to grow and improve, so if the parents are aware of a developing problem, it's to this baby and its foundation that they need to be communicating.

Actually, before getting pregnant, you can raise the intention that a good being will be born through you. Raise this intention and entrust it to your foundation. Doing this for a month before conception is fine. Or for three months is also fine.

Even if the parents didn't do anything like this before becoming pregnant, the influence of their kind and harmonious thoughts will continue to help the unborn child grow in that direction. Truly. And it even helps in the years after the child is born.

A healthy baby and attractive appearance are only a few of the many benefits of this kind of communication. This is so important and is capable of correcting many of the handicaps a child could be born with.

A while ago a pregnant woman came here in tears. She'd gone to the hospital for a checkup and received terrible news. The doctor said there was a problem with her baby, and that it would have to be delivered early by cesarean section. He added that it was unlikely the baby would survive, nor would she be able to have children again.

You can imagine how devastating this news was. On top of this, it was her first child, and both her husband and father-in-law had been only children. If she were unable to have children, there would have been immense family pressure on her husband to divorce her.

I thought about what I could say to her. She didn't know anything about how to practice, so that would have been of little use. Nor would there have been any point in telling her the reason for the baby's problems. How could that have helped the child?

So I communicated directly with the baby's foundation, and told it what it needed to do. Then, all that was needed was for it to remain inside its mother. I told her the doctor had misdiagnosed the situation, and that the baby would be fine. I said not to worry, and to start working on entrusting her wishes for the baby's health to her foundation. Some time later, she gave birth to a healthy child. In truth, the doctor hadn't been mistaken in his diagnosis.

There's nothing doctors can do for babies with that condition. While some doctors think it might be possible to cure it by treating the area around the bottom of the baby's spine, this won't work. It will fail because the essence of the problem is related to the baby's level of mind. So, to resolve the problem, the parents should communicate with the baby's foundation.

In this way, even if you encounter some dirty water, you can change it to clean water. This is also how to solve all other problems as well.

Questioner 1: My next question is about labor. When labor lasts for a long time, in about 5 percent of cases, it causes serious problems for the baby. In those cases, it's urgent that we deliver the baby immediately.

Even with an emergency cesarean section, the baby will still sometimes suffer neurological or other permanent damage. Once this happens, there's normally very little doctors can do.

So I would like to ask you, is there a way we can use our fundamental mind to help babies like this fully recover?

Kun Sunim: Quite a few mothers come to see me because their baby has developed problems while in the uterus, or because it's positioned with its head facing up. It's the baby's foundation that moves and guides it, so if we can communicate with this essence, then getting the baby turned around will be no problem.

This is why I'm always telling parents to communicate with their child. When they entrust their thoughts to their foundation, those good intentions end up being communicated to and guiding their unborn child.

This is also one of those things that's best taken care of before it becomes a problem. If the parents communicate with the baby's foundation, then this essence, this fundamental energy, will guide the baby through childbirth and make the delivery fairly easy.

If the baby puts her heels next to the placenta and pushes as she moves down and out, then the delivery will go smoothly. When the mother and the baby work together like this, then things will go well.

However, even if the baby puts its heels next to the placenta, we can't force it to push. But if through our foundation we can communicate with that child, then its foundation will guide its feet and help it to push for herself.

In other words, when the baby's essence communicates with that of its mother and the doctor, it will gain strength and won't be harmed by the delivery. And it will be born smoothly and quickly.

By the way, it's not always bad to pause during the labor and delivery. If the baby's connection with its foundation is weak, this is a good chance to reinforce that, as well as to recover its physical energy.

Ah, this spiritual strength, this ability to reflect upon our foundation and rely upon it! People lacking this seem like mannequins moving along the street. [Sighs.] This functioning of our inherent essence is just so profound and precious; words fail utterly when trying to convey a sense of this.

Questioner 1: Thank you. Kun Sunim. Next, I would like to ask about something called meconium aspiration syndrome. About 15% of babies are born having already excreted their first feces, which we call meconium. Sometimes this happens because of the pain and stress of delivery, and sometimes more naturally.

Of these babies, roughly another 15 percent have inhaled the meconium, so that it either blocks their breathing or eventually works its way deep into their lungs, where it causes all kinds of problems. Some babies die because of this, and others experience serious health problems.

As an obstetrician, I, too, had a baby die during delivery because of this. Ever since then, I've made sure to entrust the thought that my deliveries should all happen without these kinds of problems, and from that time until now, there have been no more incidents at my clinic.

When a baby excretes feces while in the womb, there's nothing we doctors can do about it except just wait until the baby is born, and hope we can clear the airway if there's a problem. Even when this works, it still can't prevent the problems that result from having meconium deep in the lungs.

I would like to know if there is anything a doctor can do to treat this, besides just entrusting positive intentions to their foundation?

Kun Sunim: What we are learning here is the truth the Buddha taught about how the world works. Actually, I can say we are learning the truth of how our minds work. And one of the things you will realize is that through this fundamental mind of ours, there are so many different skillful ways we can approach any particular situation. By entrusting the situation to our fundamental mind we can find a path that will work out.

When the parents raise a positive intention and entrust it, it is communicated to the fetus. We call this *taegyo*, or prenatal education. If parents can guide and comfort the baby like this, it won't experience any dangerous situations at all. Doctors truly need to understand this, and the possibilities it offers.

If the parents aren't practiced at communicating with the unborn child, then if that baby feels threatened, he or she will try to curl up more tightly.

And this can cause them to excrete feces, which leads to other problems. Of course, if they're curled up at the time of delivery, that's a serious problem all on its own. So, we need to focus on raising and entrusting the thought that this shouldn't happen and that the baby should be comfortable.

In the old days, midwives with these intentions for the baby put three dabs of sesame oil on the mother's head. It seems a bit silly to us now, but it contained their sincere hopes for a smooth delivery and a healthy child.

Questioner 1: Where on the head should the sesame oil be placed? In the back, or in the front?

Kun Sunim: Wherever you like. Just on the top of the head. The important thing is this essence, this foundation. That's always been with us. It's a treasure beyond treasure that has existed throughout all time. Every single one of us has this captain, no matter whether we're grown adults or unborn children. This captain is ever trying to guide us in positive directions, so if we just entrust it with whatever arises, it will never, ever lead us astray.

Questioner 1: This is my final question. Unfortunately, there are quite a few women who suffer from excessive bleeding following the delivery. Most women respond to injections of a drug type known as a uterotonic, which works to stop the bleeding, but some do not.

In those cases, surgically removing the uterus is the only option left, but some women still die before this can happen, or during the surgery. This problem in particular scares obstetricians.

These problems I've asked about today are ones that the medical field is unable to completely resolve. The longer a doctor in my field works, the more likely he or she is to encounter one of these emergencies, and the more worried they become that a patient will have one of these problems.

Of these, bleeding is the worst, and completely unpredictable. It happens very suddenly, and the blood flows like tap water. The woman's blood pressure will continue to drop sharply, and over the next ten or twenty minutes, many very, very bad things will occur.

In cases like this, I rely very heavily upon what you've taught us about raising one thought and entrusting it to our foundation. Is there anything else I should be doing? I'd be grateful for anything you could share with me.

Kun Sunim: What I've taught you isn't merely some technique, but how things actually work. Of course, "Juingong" and "foundation" are labels, and "entrust it to your foundation" is also a method, but they work towards the same, one thing: clearing the way, or opening the channel, so to speak, so that your foundation can recognize what's going on. Then, if something serious begins to appear, your foundation is able to immediately perceive it and so can respond right away.

If you are openly connected with your foundation like this, then even before the surgery, if you raise the firm determination that nothing should go wrong, then this manifests into reality.

However, this comes with one condition: you have to truly know and believe that the essence that does this is also what you truly are. You are nothing else. That which can respond fully and completely is your true nature, your true essence: that which you are now and have always been. If you miss this point, it will be difficult to completely believe in this essence. If you don't have confidence in what you truly are, how can you, as your true nature, respond confidently and completely?

A long time ago, I asked my inner self, "Where did you come from?"

It answered, "Stand up and look in a mirror." So I got up and looked in a mirror.

"The face in the mirror looks just like your face, doesn't it?"

"Yes," I replied.

My inner self continued, "Even though we have the same face, you can't say that that appearance is me, nor can I say that I am you, because in the unseen realm, I am ceaselessly changing and taking different forms. I continuously change and manifest, and the power of this is vastly beyond anything you can imagine. Discover for yourself what this truly means!"

All people have this supreme ability, but they can't use it because they think that this material self is all they are.

To put it another way, it's like the self with the physical body is the son, and the unseen self is the father. A long time ago, when I lived in the mountains, I stopped to rest next to two graves.[29] As I was leaning against one of them, I heard a voice within me say, "One grave belongs to a father, and the other to his son. If the father visits the son, both

---

29. In Korea, traditional graves are formed with a rounded mound of dirt and grass, about a meter high.

become the son; if the son visits the father, both become the father. Why is this?"

This was me teaching myself. That is to say, it was my true self teaching my present consciousness. As I reflected upon this question, the meaning became clear: the father doesn't just sit there with one shape. It manifests and takes whatever shape would be helpful. It automatically takes whatever form is needed.

Words just can't describe this. It is so strange and mysterious, yet it's truly happening all around us in our lives. This is why awakened people of old sometimes said that it was as if the *Dokkaebi*[30] were playing games with us.

If you have strong faith that your essence is working like this, there will be nothing to worry about. Just raise the thought, "There should be no problems with the delivery. From beginning to end, the entire process should go smoothly!" Make this a firm decision!

Years ago I was visited by the family of a woman who had suffered severe complications

---

30. Dokkaebi: A type of sprite or fairy from Korean folklore. In appearance they resemble ogres, and have wooden clubs that have the magical power to create things. They sometimes play tricks on bad people, but will also reward and help good people.

during childbirth. They begged me to visit her in the hospital, saying her condition was critical. So, I went to the hospital with them. It seemed that after giving birth, the woman had bled excessively; even blood vessels in her sinuses had burst and were still bleeding. The doctors had put her on a respirator, and were just barely able to keep her alive.

I entrusted the situation inwardly, and can you guess the words that arose from within me? "Will you have her released from the hospital tomorrow?" If the doctors had heard that, they would have thought I was crazy!

However, the family never hesitated and said they would. Hearing their answer, I left the hospital. Five minutes later, the bleeding stopped!

Words just can't explain this. It's something beyond them. Even though I completely understand how these things happen through the functioning of our foundation, words just can't encompass them.

Yet a single thought, raised well and entrusted to your foundation, can function like this.

Questioner 1: Thank you for such detailed answers.

Kun Sunim: This energy of our foundation.... The more we practice relying on our foundation, the more this energy becomes a great pillar that supports our life.

Questioner 2 (male): Thank you, Kun Sunim. I am a doctor, and perform many endoscopies. First, I'd like to tell you about an experience I had, and then I'll ask my question. Whenever I perform an endoscopy, I raise a thought for the patient like this, "Juingong, you're the one doing this, and the one who can make the patient comfortable. I'm just running errands in the material realm." Then I entrust this thought to my foundation.

A few days ago, before I performed an endoscopy on a patient who easily becomes nauseated, I raised a thought like this and sincerely entrusted it to my foundation. This time, "I" seemed to disappear, and the patient and I were one. From the very start, the patient had no discomfort during the procedure.

Later, I tried the same thing with other patients who had colds and digestive issues, but I couldn't feel anything, so I just raised a thought for their quick recovery. My question is this: What is the difference between those times when my mind becomes very sincere, where my sense of "me" fades away and I truly feel a connection with my patients, and those times when this feeling is completely missing?

Both times, I think I'm being equally sincere, but the first case doesn't happen very often. I wonder if I'm not actually as sincere most times, due to the lack of urgency in the patient's situation.

Kun Sunim: Once you've had those experiences of sincerely entrusting a thought and then feeling that sense of connection with your patients, you gain deeper faith in your foundation and how it works, right?

Questioner 2: Yes.

Kun Sunim: When your faith that you are already one with your foundation becomes very firm and grounded, then with just the thought that the procedure needs to go well, your energy and the energy of the whole enters the patient and works towards that outcome.

I don't mean to say that this will happen with ordinary or random thoughts. It has to be a thought entrusted so thoroughly that it becomes one with your foundation. Then it can become something that manifests into the world. Then it will function in many different ways, which you may not recognize. Sometimes it may manifest as ten or twenty doctors, working unseen to take care of the patient.

For example, suppose some part of a patient's body is failing, and surgery isn't possible, or they have some disease like leukemia where the body isn't producing enough energy. Then, through this foundation of ours, you have to enter the patient and fix the problem. In this way, you can manifest as multiple unseen doctors who go in and perform surgery. Performing surgery like this, through the unseen realm, takes just an instant.

If you keep practicing, doing the best you can with what you understand, the day will come when you truly understand the wondrous functioning that takes place when you become one with your true essence. This is sometimes called "awakening," or "attaining the way."

Regardless of the labels, this functioning of your true essence is something you need to understand and be able to apply. When you see your ordinary patients, go ahead and entrust their well-being to your foundation. However, when their situation is quite serious, you need to make a firm decision that they will turn out well. This needs to be a decision!

Questioner 2: Okay, I understand, Kun Sunim.

Kun Sunim: It's the ability to determine the direction things go. This is a great treasure that you have the potential to attain, and which you need to attain. It's something you need to practice applying across your daily life. You have to keep practicing with this until you utterly become this ability, and can use it instantly, wherever it's needed.

Even though you don't perceive it, your unseen self can transform into anything that's needed, whether seen or unseen. Through this ability it can enter the patient and treat whatever is wrong. If, after this unseen surgery, the patient's condition is unstable, your unseen self can leave behind an invisible doctor to monitor the patient and take care of them until they are okay. When your unseen self enters the patient, its form is vastly smaller than even the tiniest grain of millet, and it enters the patient without leaving any trace behind. This functioning is sometimes called the "Profound Manifestation of the Dharma."

Thus, there's nothing to worry about, nor any need to talk about what you've done. When you've become one with your foundation, you just do whatever's needed. So, work hard at trying to do this, then you can experience for yourself what I've talked about.

Questioner 2: Thank you. I will work hard at this.

Questioner 3 (male): Thank you, Kun Sunim. I'm deeply grateful for this opportunity to ask you a question. Oddly enough, you just answered the questions I came here with. I'm here though, so I'd like to ask you about two things that have been nagging me.

First, there have been several rather brutal crimes lately, which have caused a lot of commotion. To the extent that most people think about these, they feel that the cops should grab those guys and throw them away in a dark hole somewhere. However, as people who practice, it seems like we need to do more in how we raise thoughts for people who are behaving badly. So, what kinds of thoughts should I be giving rise to?

Kun Sunim: Okay, pay attention. There was a thief who would ride large ships and steal things while they sailed. He never stayed on one ship very long, and would move to a different ship before anyone could catch him.

At last, he stole things from a ship that was also carrying an awakened person. As the thief escaped on a smaller boat, the awakened person perceived what had happened. The awakened one took a careful look into the thief's past, and saw that the thief had grown up in very poor and miserable circumstances, and saw too how his actions were leading him into only more suffering. If the thief had seen this for himself, he would have never stolen a thing.

Unaware of this, he kept stealing. It became a habit, and he became entrapped in the cycle of cause and effect that arose from his actions. Of course, the deeper into this cycle he fell, the more he suffered. The thief wasn't a bad person, and didn't have a desire to harm others; he had just fallen into stealing through a series of complicated events and karmic affinities. The funny thing was, he had never been caught, not even once.

The awakened person saw all of that, and perceived that the consciousnesses urging the man to steal were relatively small and overshadowed by his general decentness. The awakened person was able to remove those consciousnesses, which then caused the man to lose his desire to steal.

If you had seen all the reasons why he was stealing, you, too, would have felt deep pity and sympathy for him. So, don't just reflexively criticize those who are behaving badly. Instead, try to understand where their behavior is coming from. If someone is hungry, if their family is starving, and stealing was the only way he could support them, then sending him to jail may not be the best option. There are other ways to keep him from stealing. Even though people like this are called thieves, they are not thieves in the true meaning of the word.

According to the law, someone who steals even a loaf of bread is a thief, and can be jailed. However, if we follow the spirit of the Buddha's teachings, we need to look into the causes underlying the theft, and then work to save everyone involved.

For example, if someone stole due to the actions of underlying states of consciousness, then if we can turn those around, they'll naturally become a good person. Or, if they stole because they're poor and hungry, we can help them earn a living on their own.

"You're a bad person, and must be punished. You're a good person, and so will be sent to a good place." This is not what the Buddha taught! The essence of the word "Bodhisattva" means working to help those destined for jail to instead find a positive path, and helping those who are going in the right direction to keep going in that direction to the very end.

It's so you can do this, that I've told you to let go of judgments of good and bad. When we let go of both "good" and "bad," our minds become free – only then can we attain the freedom to manifest as needed.

What does this mean? Well, what if I called it the energy of a ghost's fart? [Smiles.] If you can realize this, then we can save everyone. We can save everyone, unconditionally. And while doing this, we won't harm others in the slightest.

Once when I was reading the *Flower Garland Sutra*, I saw the following line. "Just walking by a Buddha results in great blessings. To hold the hand of a Buddha produces unimaginable blessings, and to look a Buddha in the face will lead to the dissolving of all the roots of evil behavior."

Can you imagine how diligently we have to work at not resenting others, at not hating them, and at not saying harsh words, in order to become a person whose presence can be such a blessing? The sutra continued, saying, "This is true, and not false – if you awaken to the truth underlying this, you will become a true Bodhisattva."

Think about this: all kinds of unpleasant things happen in order for us, or any other being, to eat, don't they? Think about all the desperate fighting that surrounds us just for the sake of eating and living.

Long ago, I was watching two bugs fight over a piece of food. Finally one of them couldn't sustain the fight any longer, and abandoned the food. It just turned around and left. I guess that humans, too, should walk away when it doesn't look like they're going to get the prize. Instead, some people keep struggling and sweating until their bodies are sick and broken. From then on, nothing in their lives is ever the same again.

So, if someone steals something and runs away, don't think, "I hope he gets arrested soon!" Instead, entrust the thought that, "Well, you've already stolen, so this time, don't get caught, but stop stealing. Going forward, live an honest life. Live a life free of fear and poverty." When you raise positive thoughts like this, it's good for the other person, and good for you as well.

Questioner 3 : Thank you. My second question is about my own circumstances. A few years ago, I started a small business. From the beginning, I raised the following thought, "I'm not the one doing this; it's my foundation that's running the business." And I made a point of letting go of the thought that "I" was doing things. But things didn't go well, and it wasn't long before I had to close the business.

I made sure to remind myself not to blame others, and in order to pay off my remaining debts, I put another building I owned up for sale. Unfortunately, it still hasn't sold, and as time goes on, the money I owe is increasing. I've been raising and entrusting the thought that, "Only my foundation, my true essence, can solve this problem."

However, worries still sometimes overwhelm me. Kun Sunim, please tell me how I can completely let go of these worries.

Kun Sunim: I think there are many people here who have experienced something similar. Every case is different, of course, but for you, things will be fine if you can just strengthen your trust in your foundation. You should have been doing things from a position of strong faith, but because your faith wavers easily, you listened to people you shouldn't have.

You didn't get mindlessly drawn into what they said, but you did believe some of it. Which led to the problems you're in. No matter what you encounter, your true self is what you need to be looking to for guidance, and where you should be asking your questions. If you're looking to others instead, only trouble will follow.

Of course, getting cheated exists there within the functioning of the truth, as does avoiding being cheated; but one will cause you hardships and suffering, so it's better to avoid it. So, before you begin something, entrust the thought that, "Only you, my foundation, can protect me from harmful things." If you entrust a firm thought like this, you'll naturally feel an aversion to locations that won't work out or people who will lead to trouble.

Next time, you need to be more firm in how you raise thoughts like these. Also, don't be so quick to completely believe what others are telling you. I'm not saying to distrust them. Trust them, care for them, but don't lose sight of your foundation.

Be careful about making people into favorites, and even if you feel like someone cheated you, don't make them into something bad or evil. Behaviors like these are why your business problem happened. They created an atmosphere ripe for gossiping and scheming, which, without you being aware of it, gave rise to the problems that caused your bankruptcy.

So, next time, be more careful, and start by firmly entrusting the thought to your foundation that, "It's you that can make this business go well." You also need to be sure to raise this kind of thought about finishing things well. And when you finish, there's all kinds of reasons why it's hard to give something back, aren't there? So, before you even begin, make a firm decision to give something back when you finish.

Questioner 4 (male): Thank you for this opportunity to ask you a question. During one of your Dharma talks, you told us the story of a man who was walking along a road when he encountered a cow. As soon as he saw the cow, he suddenly understood that this was his brother, reborn. So he put his brother's spirit within his own body and became one with him.

You then asked us to do this when we encounter beings we have a prior connection with, who have been reborn in unfortunate circumstances. We should absorb them into our foundation and live together. But, and this is my question, how does this work? It almost sounds like what shamans and psychics do, when they invite a spirit into their body so that they can use its ability.

Kun Sunim: As for how it works, when it comes to your Juingong, it clearly exists, yet whether others perceive it or not depends upon the depth of their own practice. So, sometimes practitioners would test each other, saying things like, "Have you grasped the seed of a ghost's fart?[31] If you have, are you able to go out and play with a ball?"[32]

Even though you put 10,000 ghosts into this foundation, they become one with our foundation in an instant. Even though you send forth 10,000 beings from this place, it happens in an instant. Earlier, a doctor asked about surgery, right? If there were one hundred people needing surgery, your foundation could easily manifest one hundred invisible doctors that would enter them and perform the surgeries. This is how your foundation works: instantly, entering and leaving, taking things in or out, and doing it all without leaving any trace.

---

31. Here, a "ghost's fart" is a way of saying "nothing."

32. In Korean, the word for "ball" is a homophone with "emptiness."

Among you, there are probably people who had parents or ancestors who didn't know about spiritual practice, and who also lived hard, brutal lives. If it occurs to you that it would be good for those spirits to practice together with you, then invite them to join you. Even though they combine with you, they won't cause you any problems at all. Likewise, they'll leave no traces behind as they learn, nor as they leave to be reborn. If they want to tell you something about what's going on with them, they may do it through dreams or something similar.

You might be scared or unsettled by what you experience, but don't be, because practicing together like this is good for everyone involved. By shedding one shape after another for eons, you've already evolved to the point where you can have a human body. So don't let yourself be scared by those kinds of things; that's not the path to becoming a true human being.

Having come this far, we have to dissolve the habits of this level as well. Only then can we reach higher levels and truly live as one with others, having the ability to solve any problem we come across.

Questioner 4: My second question is about my own experience, and whether there are any aspects of it I need to handle better.

Late last year, I began to have some difficulties breathing. This often woke me up during the night, so I really wasn't sleeping well, either. I found some medicine that helped me breathe better, but as soon as I stopped taking it, the problem returned.

I went to the hospital, but the doctors there said that I was fine. So I went to an oriental medicine clinic, and those treatments worked for a while. But within a few months the problem returned. Then I remembered something you said, and raised the thought that, "Only you, my true essence, can make me healthy," and entrusted it to my foundation. Still, I was afraid, and thought that perhaps I should go to a bigger hospital for in-depth testing.

In the meantime, I'd gotten some cassette tapes of your teachings, and was listening to them. You said, "Even though you are sick, don't be worried about possible bad things that might happen. Have firm faith in your foundation and entrust it with all of your anxieties and fears. Just go forward trusting it, regardless of whether you live or die."

When I heard this, the unrest within me suddenly disappeared. I felt very deeply that if I firmly relied upon my foundation, then it would take care of things and show me the way. If my condition were something that could be fixed without a doctor, then that would happen. And if I needed to see a doctor, then my foundation would lead me to a hospital.

I felt very confident in this, and the stress and tension in me drained away. This happened shortly after lunch, and I began to feel drowsy and took a nap. I slept for 20 minutes or so, and when I awoke, I felt really good. Ever since then, I've felt great, and have had no problems breathing. Is there anything I've overlooked or need to do differently going forward?

Kun Sunim: That's not all. You heard earlier of all the difficulties and dangers that pregnant women can experience, right? You all have a body that experiences all kinds of suffering as well, don't you? I do, too, because I have a body.

However, it's not this body that causes us to live, but rather our true self that enables our bodies to live. It is the captain within you that sustains and guides your flesh. The Buddha, too, once talked about this, using the metaphor of a ship. A storm arose, with wind and waves, and tossed a ship about. The people on board began to panic and cry, but there was one person who stayed calm and entrusted the situation to his foundation. As he did this, the waves became calm and the winds died away.

You have to believe in yourself! Of all the people and things in this world, you as your true self are what you have to believe in! Even if Buddha were sitting right here, whether he becomes one with you and works together with you would depend upon your mind. If your thoughts are generous and broad-minded, then Buddha will work together with you generously and compassionately. Whether this happens or not depends upon your thoughts.

If you work hard at raising kind and generous thoughts, even though difficulties and terrifying things happen, they won't be able to touch your heart, for the thoughts you give rise to manifest into the world. Everything in the world begins with our thoughts, and those thoughts always begin within us.

Thus, if you want to go forward in your life unbowed and with a smile, don't cling to yesterday's things, nor worry about what will come tomorrow, nor even about living itself. If you start dwelling on these things, they will become the focus of all your thoughts, and leave room for little else.

Much of your suffering comes from your habits, and if you keep worrying, that, too, will become a habit. You'll be worried and stressed over things you don't need to be concerned about. So, as much as possible, let go of your worries and live with a smile and a laugh.

I feel a little bad that my Dharma talks are so serious, and don't give you much of a chance for a good laugh. We are all fully capable of living with joy and laughter, so why aren't we? Because we exist, we encounter all kinds of different experiences and problems, but all of those can be solved by viewing them wisely and entrusting that to our foundation.

Even with problems of the natural world, the thoughts we give rise to can solve those, or make them much worse. This is why I'm always saying you have to be careful in how you raise thoughts. Even while deep in the mountains, if you raise a thought wisely, you will be given food and shelter.

Questioner 5 (male): It's wonderful to see you like this, but I see that we are behind schedule, so I'll be brief.

Kun Sunim: Relax, and sit comfortably. Even if someone tries to hit you with a stick, you need to be able to remain unshaken and do what you came for.

Questioner 5: Thank you. First, I'd like to ask you about a dream I had a few days ago. You showed up in my dream, affectionately stroked my head as if I were a small child, saying, "Tomorrow is my birthday," and left. In my dream, I wanted to buy you a cake, and was about to go order a three-tier cake for you. At that point, I woke up, and have been wondering about this dream ever since.

Kun Sunim: [Laughs.] Thank you! But instead of giving me that cake, you should be able to eat and enjoy it yourself. Now, the three tiers: You lived yesterday, you will live tomorrow, and you're living now, but all of those form one ceaselessly flowing whole. If you can view all things nondualistically, and if you can do everything from this foundation, while letting go of any trace of "me" or "I," then great wisdom will arise.

Questioner 5: Thank you. Second, I'd like to ask you about a thought that arose within me: "Within me questions are asked without speaking, and answered without speaking. But they are both still one. Why is this?"

Kun Sunim: We're functioning like that right now, aren't we? Within us right now, speaking, answering, giving, and receiving are all happening as one flowing whole. However, to truly realize this for yourself, you need to be the one to eat that cake, instead of trying to give it to me.

To put it another way, you need to take everything that arises and feed it back to your foundation. When you can do this, all of your parents and ancestors will be connected there and share in that cake together.

Questioner 5: Thank you. When I lined up to ask you a question, I was the fifth person, and was told that only four people could ask questions today because of the time. But I firmly raised the thought that I wanted to ask you my questions, and it turned out so.

Kun Sunim: Yes, go forward like that.

Sometimes people tend to give up before even trying, don't they? Just the other day, a man said to me, "This thing I have to do will fail anyway; there's no point in even raising a positive thought. It's such a bad situation that I don't know why I'm even bothering you with it."

So I said to him, "That which you think is possible or not is nothing more than your own guesses and habits of thinking. Leave all those behind! The truth of what the Buddha taught is having faith in the great interconnected energy and flowing of everything, and then deciding, from this very deep place, which way things need to go."

When something very urgent arises, like if your company is about to go bankrupt, then firmly decide how you need things to go, and entrust that to your foundation. In this way, you can prevent the situation from getting worse, and gain time to minimize the damage.

Anyway, you all should deeply understand this principle. I meet a lot of people every day, and see how important it is that everyone understands this. That's why I keep talking about it.

My experiences may seem like something from another age to young people today, but having lived as a woman, I've met so many women who led desperately unhappy and unfortunate lives because they were unaware of this ability within them. Some of them even took their own lives. Many others wanted to be reborn as men in their next lives because of their suffering. I haven't always been born as a woman, but this time I chose to be born with a plain-looking, female shape. A very plain shape was needed to accomplish my goal.

You need to think like this: "I believe in the captain, my true self, who is guiding me. This captain is the best. When the situation is urgent, this captain manifests in all kinds of different ways to take care of me." This is important; whether you are good looking or not just isn't. When you have this kind of firm faith in your foundation and entrust everything to it, it will guide and take care of not only you, but also the people in your life that you are close to.

A few years ago a man came here and asked me a question: "My brothers and I have been having horrible fights, with people even hitting each other and throwing things. We have to get together for various family memorial services, and this fighting has just about destroyed our family. What can I do to change this?"

Even these days, there are many people here who don't understand this truth of their fundamental mind, but back in those days there were many more who didn't understand it. Well, I could see that even though I told him exactly what to do, he wouldn't be able to follow through with that. I realized that I would have to be the one to run this errand between the seen and unseen realms. So I told him, "I understand, I'll do my job," and he left feeling much relieved. A while later, I heard that the brothers had reconciled, and that the whole family had become much more harmonious.

Even though your life is tough right now, you have to practice diligently so that you can do these kinds of things for yourself. Practice during this one life such that the benefits of that will last across all your future lives. Practice such that you will forever be able to live freely, and freely make use of the great ability inherent within you.

Everyone here loves and cares for their children, but have you ever thought about where your children are headed after this life? Have you ever wondered about what path their future lives will take? What shape they'll have, what spiritual level they'll be living at? Even when those who were once your parents are reborn as your own children, you can't see this, can you? So, don't look down upon anyone, not your parents, not your children, not anyone. Nor even upon those who have passed away.

Some of our centers have stupa parks for deceased family members and ancestors, don't they? The sunims there clean and wash the stupas once a year, as if they were their own. Who are those people in the stupas? They aren't strangers. The sunims aren't doing this for the money.

When we let go of distinctions between ourselves and others, becoming one with them all as we entrust them, and "me," to our foundation, we will attain the great way and be able to live freely, life after life. We will be able to use the infinite ability within each of us to help whoever is in need. Let's all do this together!

GLOSSARY

Avalokitesvara Bodhisattva (觀世音菩薩):
The Bodhisattva of Compassion, who hears and responds to the cries of the world and delivers unenlightened beings from suffering.

Bhikkuni:
Female sunims who are fully ordained are called Bhikkuni (比丘尼) sunims, while male sunims who are fully ordained are called Bhikku (比丘) sunims. This can also be a polite way of indicating male or female sunims.

Bodhisattva:
In the most basic sense, Bodhisattva is the applied energy of our fundamental nature, used to help save beings. It can also be described as the non-dual wisdom of enlightenment being used to help beings awaken for themselves. It is also depicted as a person of great spiritual ability who is dedicated to saving those lost in ignorance and suffering.

Buddha:
In this text, "Buddha" and "Bodhisattva" are capitalized out of respect, because these represent the essence and function of the enlightened mind. "The Buddha" always refers to Sakyamuni Buddha.

Buddha-dharma:

In general this refers to the fundamental reality that the teachings of Buddha point towards, but it occasionally means the teachings themselves.

Dharma:

This refers to both ultimate truth, and the truth taught by the Buddha.

Dharma Realm:

The level of reality where everything functions as an interpenetrated and connected whole. Daehaeng Kun Sunim said that this can also be called the Dharma net, and compared it to our circulatory system, which connects and nourishes every single cell in the body.

Doing without any thought of doing:

While this can mean thought and action free of any sense of a separate "me" or "I" that's doing things, it also means letting go of the thought that "I" did something or experienced something, once we become aware of that train of thought.

Dokkaebi:

A type of sprite or fairy from Korean folklore. In appearance they resemble ogres, and have wooden clubs that have the magical power to create things. They sometimes play tricks on bad people, but will also reward and help good people.

Five subtle powers (五神通):
These are the power to know past and future lives, the power to know others' thoughts and emotions, the power to see anything, the power to hear anything, and the power to go anywhere.

Habits (習):
These include not just the ways of thought and behavior learned in this life, but also all of those tendencies of thought and behavior that have accumulated over endless eons.

Hanmaum [han-ma-um]:
"Han" means one, great, and combined, while "maum" means mind, as well as heart, and together they mean everything combined and connected as one. What is called "Hanmaum" is intangible, unseen, and transcends time and space. It has no beginning or end, and is sometimes called our fundamental mind. It also means the mind of all beings and everything in the universe connected and working together as one. In English, we usually translate this as "one mind."

Interdependent arising / dependent arising:
The idea that all things arise according to, or are dependent on, other things.

Juingong (主人空):

Pronounced "ju-in-gong." Juin (主人) means the true doer or the master, and gong (空) means "empty." Thus Juingong is our true nature, our true essence, the master within that is always changing and manifesting, without a fixed form or shape.

Daehaeng Sunim has compared Juingong to the root of the tree. Our bodies and consciousness are like the branches and leaves, but it is the root that is the source of the tree, and it is the root that sustains the visible tree.

Karmic affinity (因緣):

The connection or attraction between people or things, due to previous karmic relationships.

Kasyapa, or Mahakasyapa:

Regarded as the foremost of the ten great disciples of the Buddha. He was well known for his self discipline, and the Buddha himself praised Kasyapa for his attainment and realization. After the Buddha's passing, Kasyapa was chosen to lead the great council that gathered to record the teachings of the Buddha.

Ksitigarbha Bodhisattva (地藏菩薩):

The guardian of the earth who is devoted to saving all beings from suffering, and especially those beings lost in the hell realms.

Manjushri (文殊):
The Bodhisattva who represents the essence of wisdom. Manjushri is traditionally portrayed holding the sword of wisdom in his right hand, and in his left hand holds a blue lotus that represents the flowering of wisdom, while riding a lion that represents courage and majesty.

Mind (Kor. –maum) (心):
In Mahayana Buddhism, "mind" refers to this fundamental mind, and almost never means the brain or intellect. It is intangible, beyond space and time, and has no beginning or end. It is the source of everything, and everyone is endowed with it.

The Northern Dipper (Also known as the Big Dipper.):
Traditionally in Korea, people have believed that the seven stars of the Northern Dipper govern the length of humans' lives.

One mind (Hanmaum [han-ma-um]):
From the Korean, where "one" has a nuance of great and combined, while "mind" is more than intellect and includes "heart" as well. Together, they mean everything combined and connected as one. What is called "one mind" is intangible, unseen, and transcends time and space. It has no beginning or end, and is sometimes called our fundamental mind. It also means the mind of all beings and everything in the universe connected and working together as one.

Seon (Chan, Zen) (禪):

Seon describes the unshakable state where one has firm faith in their inherent foundation, their Buddha-nature, and so returns everything they encounter back to this fundamental mind. It also means letting go of "I," "me," and "mine" throughout one's daily life.

Sunim / **Kun Sunim**:

Sunim is the respectful title for a Buddhist monk or nun in Korea, and Kun Sunim is the title given to outstanding nuns or monks.

Other Books by Seon Master Daehaeng

<u>English</u>

• Wake Up And Laugh (Wisdom Publications)
• No River To Cross (Wisdom Publications)
• My Heart Is A Golden Buddha (Hanmaum Publications)
• Touching The Earth (Hanmaum Publications)
• A Thousand Hands of Compassion (Hanmaum Publications)
• One Mind: Principles (Hanmaum Publications)

<u>Korean/English</u>

• A Thousand Hands of Compassion (Hanmaum Publications)
  [received *2010 iF communication design Award*]
• Practice in Daily Life (Korean/English bilingual series)
  1. To Discover Your True Self, "I" Must Die
  2. Walking Without A Trace
  3. Let Go And Observe
  4. Mind, Treasure House Of Happiness
  5. The Furnace Within Yourself
  6. The Spark That Can Save The Universe
  7. The Infinite Power Of One Mind
  8. In The Heart Of A Moment
  9. One With The Universe
  10. Protecting The Earth
  11. Inherent Connections
  12. Finding A Way Forward
  13. Faith In Action

<u>Korean</u>

• 건널 강이 어디 있으랴 (Hanmaum Publications)
• 내 마음은 금부처 (Hanmaum Publications)
• 처음 시작하는 마음공부1 (Hanmaum Publications)

<u>Russian</u>

• Дзэн И Просветление (Amrita-Rus)

German

- Wache Auf und Lache (Theseus)
- Umarmt von Mitgefühl (Deutsch·Koreanisch, Diederichs)
- Wie fließendes Wasser (Goldmann)
- Wie fließendes Wasser - CD (Steinbach sprechende bücher)
- Vertraue und lass alles los (Goldmann)

Spanish

- Ningún Río Que Cruzar (Kailas Editorial)
- Una Semilla Inherente Alimenta El Universo
  (Hanmaum Publications)
- Si Te Lo Propones, No Hay Imposibles (Hanmaum Publications)
- El Camino Interior (Hanmaum Publications)
- Vida De La Maestra Seon Daehaeng (Hanmaum Publications)
- Enseñanzas De La Maestra Daehaeng (Hanmaum Publications)

Czech

- Probuď se! (Eugenika)

Indonesian

- Sup Cacing Tanah (PT Gramedia)

Vietnamese

- Không có sông nào để vượt qua
  (Hanmaum Publications, Korea / Vien Chieu, Vietnam)

Chinese

- 我心是金佛 (简体字) (Hanmaum Publications, Korea)
- 我心是金佛 (繁体字) (橡树林文化出版, Taiwan)
- 无河可渡 (简体字) (Hanmaum Publications, Korea)
- 人生不是苦海 (繁体字) (Hanmaum Publications, Korea)

Anyang Headquarters of Hanmaum Seonwon

1282 Gyeongsu-daero, Manan-gu, Anyang-si,
Gyeonggi-do, 13908, Republic of Korea
Tel: (82-31) 470-3175 / Fax: (82-31) 470-3209
www.hanmaum.org/eng
onemind@hanmaum.org

Overseas Branches of Hanmaum Seonwon

ARGENTINA
Buenos Aires
Miró 1575, CABA, C1406CVE, Rep. Argentina
Tel: (54-11) 4921-9286 / Fax: (54-11) 4921-9286
http://hanmaumbsas.org

Tucumán
Av. Aconquija 5250, El Corte, Yerba Buena,
Tucumán, T4107CHN, Rep. Argentina
Tel: (54-381) 425-1400
www.hanmaumtuc.org

BRASIL
São Paulo
R. Newton Prado 540, Bom Retiro
Sao Paulo, CEP 01127-000, Brasil
Tel: (55-11) 3337-5291
www.hanmaumbr.org

CANADA
Toronto
20 Mobile Dr., North York, Ontario M4A 1H9, Canada
Tel: (1-416) 750-7943
www.hanmaum.org/toronto

GERMANY
Kaarst
Broicherdorf Str. 102, 41564 Kaarst, Germany
Tel: (49-2131) 969551 / Fax: (49-2131) 969552
www.hanmaum-zen.de

THAILAND
Bangkok
86/1 Soi 4 Ekamai Sukhumvit 63
Bangkok, Thailand
Tel: (66-2) 391-0091
www.hanmaum.org/cafe/thaihanmaum

USA
Chicago
7852 N. Lincoln Ave., Skokie, IL 60077, USA
Tel: (1-847) 674-0811
www.hanmaum.org/chicago

Los Angeles
1905 S. Victoria Ave., L.A., CA 90016, USA
Tel: (1-323) 766-1316
www.hanmaum.org/la

New York
144-39, 32 Ave., Flushing, NY 11354, USA
Tel: (1-718) 460-2019 / Fax: (1-718) 939-3974
www.juingong.org

Washington D.C.
7807 Trammel Rd., Annandale, VA 22003, USA
Tel: (1-703) 560-5166
www.hanmaum.org/wa

If you would like more information about these books or
would like to order copies of them,
please call or write to:

Hanmaum International Culture Institute
Hanmaum Publications
1282 Gyeongsu-daero, Manan-gu, Anyang-si,
Gyeonggi-do, 13908,
Republic of Korea
Tel: (82-31) 470-3175
Fax: (82-31) 470-3209
e-mail: onemind@hanmaum.org
www.hanmaumbooks.org

Made in the USA
Middletown, DE
21 March 2020